D1459627

AMAZON

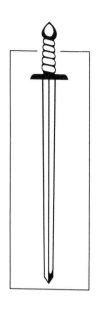

AMAZON
A NOVEL

BARBARA G. WALKER

HarperSanFrancisco
A Division of HarperCollins*Publishers*

TEXT DESIGN BY WENDY CALMENSON, THE BOOK COMPANY

FIRST EDITION

Library of Congress Cataloging-in-Publication Data

Walker, Barbara G.
    Amazon : a novel / Barbara G. Walker.
        p. cm.
    I. Title.
    ISBN 0-06-250975-6
    PS3573.A42516A83 1992   91-58145
    813'.54—dc20   CIP

---

92 93 94 95 96 MART 10 9 8 7 6 5 4 3 2 1

This edition is printed on acid-free paper that meets the American National Standards Institute Z39.48 Standard.

AMAZON

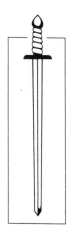

CHAPTER 1

U<small>NDER THE</small> G<small>ODDESS-GIVEN LAWS OF MY MOTHERCLAN,</small> a warrior woman was not allowed to choose a husband and bear children until she had achieved her first kill in battle. Most of our women accomplished this before reaching the age of twenty. I, however, did not manage to kill a Greek until I was twenty-four.

By that time I had taken part in many battles. I had inflicted wounds and had suffered them. But the Goddess did not give me an individual victim until the battle of the high meadow, in the winter of my twenty-fifth year.

The Greeks had come down on us in force, burning two border villages and slaughtering most of the motherclans there. Three women escaped, after seeing all their children murdered. They caught two horses and galloped all night to spread the alarm. By dawn, warriors from half the countryside were mobilized. Both women and men gathered by the south temple to ride forth as the first rays of the sun pierced the dark green towers of the pines.

I rode beside Antheos, my most recent lover. We grinned at each other as our horses trotted into the bright morning mist. I liked Antheos. He was a good, sturdy, tireless fighter, as I knew from many practice duels with him. He was also a good enough lover, though not the sort of man I would choose to help raise my children. We were comfortable together as comrades-in-arms, if not passionately devoted. Our warrior training left us little energy for the softer passions, in any case.

The pleasures of that morning were brief but keen: the jingling and creaking of harnesses; the rich smells of leather, horses, and dewy earth; the glittering sunlight on massed spears and helmets; the communal joy of strong young people riding forth to meet a challenge together. I was deeply moved by feelings of loyalty to my clansisters and clanbrothers: we were one in our hearts; we would die for one another. These feelings were enhanced by the beauty of the day, the sweet fresh air, and the satisfying sense of healthy muscles in motion.

I leaned over to stroke the sleek neck of Windeater, my dear black mare. She shook her head and snorted, prancing a little to show that she too felt the joy of the morning. The horses were excited, almost as excited as their riders. My people understood the feelings of horses; the Greeks did not. They did not know how to raise and train a horse so that she would carry her rider willingly and with love.

The Greeks painted grotesque pictures of us without our legs, our torsos ending in horse bodies. They thought we had a secret magic that made us part animal. It is true that we had a magic, but it was no secret. It was only kindness. The Greeks couldn't understand this, for kindness was not much known or practiced among them.

This fact struck us forcibly about midday, when we came upon the first of the devastated villages. The crops were trampled and ruined. Houses were heaps of smoking rubble. Dead bodies lay everywhere. I saw several babies and small children sliced in half from crotch to neck—a typical Greek atrocity. They also did this to women after raping them.

As we rode through the wreckage, our ebullient mood faded away and was replaced by a grim rage. When we found the Greek camp a few miles farther on, in the high meadow, we charged into it like the Furies themselves.

Our attack was unexpected. Thinking our warriors far away, the Greeks were relaxing, eating and drinking, idly tormenting prisoners, or enjoying their sadistic sexual games. They had posted no guards; their raiding party greatly outnumbered our forces, and this had given them false confidence. The surprise gave us an advantage, and our horses, as always, gave us the tactical advantages of speed and leverage.

The Greeks still did not know how to ride in battle. They used only packhorses: poor, tortured, half-crippled, spiritless beasts accustomed to chains, whips, and heavy burdens. The Greeks liked to make slaves of horses and humans alike.

Our first charge disabled almost a third of the Greek foot soldiers. Our women and men fought like lions. We galloped through the camp, striking down foes on every side. In disarray, they began to flee in all directions. A few of their leaders raised their banners to gather their troops around them. Pockets of resistance began to form.

We knew enough to attack these groups before they could grow in strength. We had learned from bitter experience that the Greeks were no cowards. Cruel and vile they might be, but they were also expert and willing fighters. Our whole country might have been overwhelmed by them generations ago had not the wisdom of our foremothers decreed warrior training for all our young people.

I had charged into one of these clusters and was busy striking furiously on each side when I caught sight of Antheos some distance away, in an open space near the meadow's edge. He was surrounded by four Greeks who had seized his horse and were trying to pull him off its back. One of the Greeks had cut

Antheos's leg severely. Another had stabbed his horse's belly. The animal was plunging in terror and pain, trying to free itself, while Antheos was struggling to control it and to strike his attackers at the same time.

I could not ride at once to his rescue. I was engaged with a tall, fat-bellied Greek who came swinging a heavy hammer at Windeater's leg, trying to cripple her. He missed. It was his last chance. I struck the side of his head with all my might. Off balance, he slipped in the trampled mud and fell. Windeater's forefoot came down squarely on his neck and broke it.

I wondered about this later. I knew that horses would not step on human beings if they could avoid doing so. Perhaps Windeater did not have time to choose another spot for her hoof, or perhaps she was becoming a warrior just like me. Alas, I will never know the answer now. But whether inadvertently or otherwise, she did kill her first Greek that day.

Seconds later I saw that Antheos's horse was down and was pinning Antheos's wounded leg under its shoulder. Shrilling my battle cry, calling upon the Mother, I left the thick of the fight and charged to the aid of my lover. I saw Antheos stab upward with his sword and give one of his opponents a mortal wound. While he was trying to pull his blade from the first man's body, a second one leapt on him and plunged a sword deep into his chest. Still pinned under his horse, Antheos died as I was galloping to save him.

From the corner of my eye I saw my clansister Niobe on her yellow stallion, also galloping to the rescue. I rode past two of the remaining Greeks, leaving them to her, while I slashed Antheos's killer between his neck and collarbone. This was a mistake: I should not have turned my back on the other two Greeks. Niobe did indeed kill them both, but not before one of them had cut the hocks of my brave Windeater and hamstrung her. I didn't realize what had happened until her hindquarters sagged to the ground and spilled me from her back.

Fortunately I landed on my feet. Physically I was unhurt, but I was wounded in my soul. Two beings who had been my faithful and joyous companions only that morning were now taken from my life. Overcome by grief and horror, I watched my beautiful mare groveling like a crushed worm in the bloody mud, throwing her head about and screaming. I knew what I had to do. My heart was bursting with the pain of it.

Heedless of everything except my sorrow, I pulled Windeater's head against my body and held her as firmly as I could. Despite her pain, she calmed. She trusted me to help her. After all, I had cared for her ever since she was a wobbly-kneed foal.

As gently as possible, I stretched her throat and gave her the deadly slice straight across the artery. Her heavy head sagged in my arms, drenching me with her blood. Tears streamed down my cheeks as I laid her head on the ground and automatically smoothed the tangled hairs of her mane for the last time.

I felt the weight of a gaze on my back. Turning, I found the killer of Antheos propped up on one elbow, watching me. He was dying, and he knew it; but he was calm. A brave man.

We stared into each other's eyes. His eyes were a curious golden hazel color, clear as jewels. He was young, handsome, delicate-featured, not a long-nosed brute like most Greeks. He opened his lips as if he would speak to me, but no voice would come from his mutilated throat.

My sorrowful rage was so great that I wanted to strike him again, to kill him twice over. Yet for a moment I felt pity for him, the same pity that I had felt for my mare. At the same time I reminded myself that pity for an enemy is inappropriate in a warrior. My sword was raised to strike him. He saw the blow coming. He did not move. His strange golden eyes held mine to the last second of his life. As my arm was descending, his body flattened down to the earth and he died. My blow never landed, and those strange golden eyes never closed. Even in death they seemed to watch me. As I walked away, I was still aware of their dead gaze at my back.

The battle was almost over.

Niobe was there, leading her stallion toward me. She too was unwounded. She held me in her arms while I cried for the waste of life, for my own bereavements, and for the aftermath of powerful emotions. The Greek raiders were nearly all dead. A remnant fled into the woods. Our warriors chased them and cut down most of them. Perhaps a few managed to hide and escape, but they were not heard of again. Our battle priestesses took the omens and predicted that we would be safe from Greek marauders for a long time. Our people had won a great victory.

The Goddess was good to us that day. And although She deprived me of two of my dearest companions, She preserved me in good health. Looking back on my experiences, I sometimes wish that She had not kept me so carefully unharmed, only to undergo all the trials that were to come and that no one in my motherclan—or even in my entire country—could ever have imagined.

First killing of an enemy in battle constituted a rite of passage for our women. For me it was more. It was the beginning of a life so strange that even now I can hardly believe it happened.

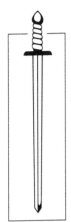

CHAPTER 2

THREE DAYS BEFORE THE NEXT MOON-DYING, I BEGAN the ritual fast to prepare for my pilgrimage to holy Themiskyra, the site of the central temple that all the motherclans knew to be the womb of creation and the source of the Mother's power. Up to that time we had all been busy, rebuilding and repopulating the border villages, retrieving what we could of their provisions, and collecting the valuable iron swords from the Greek dead. Iron was the most precious of metals, rare among us. Our smiths needed to study it and learn more about the working of it.

We also instituted funeral games to mourn our dead and pass them back to the Mother. Even though we knew they would return someday, it was hard to say farewell to loved ones, knowing that we might not see them again in this life. I was particularly grieved by the loss of my Windeater. I felt sure that her equine body had housed what was once a human soul. I had no other horse, so I would have to make the journey to Themiskyra on foot.

I had visited the central temple only once before in my life, when my moonblood came upon me for the first time. I was very young then, of course, and mightily impressed by the

7

solemnity of the occasion. The priestesses had bathed and adorned me, taught me some of the Mysteries, and led me into the presence of the Goddess and Her current god-consort in a cavern lit only by the perpetual fire. I was moved to tears by the honor of my assimilation to the Mother spirit through Her unmistakable touch on my womb. I could never again observe the full moon without feeling a hint of that reverence.

In our country, a warrior woman made her second visit to the great temple after her first kill. There she would be purged of blood guilt, released from responsibility to her victim's ghost, and made ready for her new life phase as matron and mother, with the Goddess-given power to establish her own clan. I knew that as part of the ritual, I would incubate for three nights of moondeath in the Mother's holy womb. When the crescent of the Maiden rose in the sky, I would be born again.

It was a privilege to enter that temple, which housed the holy of holies: the Black Stone, sent from heaven by the Mother. Themiskyra's Black Stone was kept in the womb cave at the core of the world, guarded by the priestesses who were the world's holiest women. The temple facade was built against the natural hill that gave entrance to the caves. Although our foremothers had dwelt in this land since Pyrrha's divine blood had first animated the stones, there were still portions of the sacred caves that no human eye had seen. It was said that each priestess studied the underground labyrinth for many moons before she learned enough of its ways to walk there alone.

In the temple antechamber, I stripped off all my garments, leaving only my sword belt and sword and the small goatskin bag that hung from my neck, containing my amulets. A warrior woman does not lay aside these items for any reason whatsoever. Then a priestess helped me to bathe, purify, and perfume myself. She combed and braided my hair, anointed me with holy oil, and drew the Star of Knowledge on my forehead with Tyrian purple dye. I knelt on the stone floor at the entrance to the labyrinth, shivering a little in the morning chill, while the priestess fetched another torch to lead me down to the womb of my rebirth.

One does not forget a journey into the sacred caves. Every detail of that trip is imprinted on my mind. The priestess and I passed a series of niches containing various carved and painted representations of the Mother and Her incarnations, the heroines of legend, the ancestral queens and their kings, the clan-mothers, and the saints. Small votive lamps burned before each, appearing and disappearing like stars in the darkness as we walked along. In some niches there were great carved images of gigantic size, glittering with gems and precious metals. In others there were living women, members of the priestesshood, masked and costumed to depict certain religious principles and entities. To these I made obeisance, while they performed ritual gestures and asked me special questions to which I made the required responses. These are holy Mysteries that I may not describe in detail.

I was shown the chamber of the Black Stone. The priestess drew aside a curtain and allowed me to look into the shrine, although I was not allowed to enter. I opened my amulet bag and took out my eye stone. I held it up so that it might look its fill upon the divine Stone from the stars; and might become saturated with the power of that Stone, so that my eye stone's gift of seeing would never fail me. When I returned my eye stone to its place, it seemed to radiate a warmth that I could feel even through the goatskin.

There were many other natural wonders to be seen in the labyrinth. The priestess's torch revealed wondrous shapes of stone: knives, waterfalls, nests of serpents, and caryatids. Crystals sparkled like star-seed in the dark. Here and there were pools like black mirrors. The rocks were of many colors. Some, indeed, had even been painted by our foremothers, who had illuminated the cave walls with magical picture charms for hunting, planting, or birthing.

At last we arrived at the yoni door that had been chosen for my rebirthing, deep in the bowels of Mother Earth. The door was a small vulva-shaped opening, partly natural, partly sculpted, wide enough to admit an adult human body. The opening was faced with wool fleeces dyed blood red and faintly damp. Inside, the hole was totally black but not stale. The air smelled fresh enough.

The priestess said, "Here you will crawl in, just as you once crawled out of your mother. I will seal the door behind you." She indicated the heavy stone slab that would cover the opening and be secured with wooden bolts once I was inside. "Fear not, Antiope," she said. "You will be as comfortable as in your first womb. There will be pure air for you to breathe, entering through small shafts. There is water for you to drink, as you drank the fluids of your mother. There is a deep hole, leading down to the bottomless abyss, where you may deposit your wastes. But as you are fasting, you will have few excrements. Rest and meditate. Try to return to the fetal state. Perhaps a great vision will come to you."

I bowed my head, and she stroked my hair thoughtfully. "The traveling of your soul will be long," she said. "I cannot see where it will end. I think you will be in some danger, dear Antiope. But you are brave and strong. You have faced danger before."

"Yes," I answered. I did not feel afraid. The labyrinth, the uterine caves, the interior of Mother Earth's body seemed to me more hospitable than otherwise. What evil could come to me in the womb of my Mother?

I kissed the priestess and received her blessing. Then I crawled through the yoni door and entered the passage beyond. This too had been lined with red-dyed fleeces. The glow of the priestess's torch disappeared as she closed the opening behind me and secured the bolts with a hollow booming sound. I was enveloped in absolute blackness, in a silence so thick that I could hear my own blood in my ears. I experienced a brief moment of panic as I felt the adamant rigidity of the rock pressing all about me, just behind the deceptive softness of the fleece. I stopped to breathe quietly and calm myself. Then I went on, lying on my belly, pulling myself along by my elbows. After another twenty feet or so, I came to the womb chamber.

Here I could stand erect, although the ceiling was no more than a foot above my head. With outstretched arms I could touch both walls. The space was just large enough for me to stand, sit, or lie down as I chose. The whole chamber was padded with soft fleeces attached firmly to the rock. It felt damp and chilly at first, but I knew that my body heat would soon warm it. I found the air holes, each about three fingers wide, and the waste hole. In the corner farthest from the entry, a trickle of water came out of the rock to fill a small stone hollow that had been naturally or artificially shaped like a cup. From this vessel I could drink the Mother's pure amniotic waters whenever I wished. I tasted the water; it was sweet and cool.

At first I found the impenetrable blackness more oppressive than I had expected. Seated, I centered and composed myself until the oppression lifted. Then I began to see lights and images inside my eyelids.

The likeness of my victim arose unexpectedly before my inner sight. I saw again the last desperate stare of his golden hazel eyes. Surely his ghost could not torment me here, in this sacred place! As a charm against possible spiritual hostility, I took my amulets out of their bag and held them, two to each hand. I did not have to see them. I knew them well by touch.

There were four of them, each one magically linked to one of the elements. The first was my Maiden stone, as colorless and clear as the water she represented, a sharp six-sided crystal of the quartz that the Greeks call *krystallos*, meaning petrified ice. The second was my Mother stone, a heart-shaped polished carnelian as red as the element of fire; this was my stone of sexuality, passion, and of a fighting spirit as indomitable as that of a mother defending the children she has formed of her heart's blood. The third was my Crone stone, as black as the bowels of the earth in which I was now buried—a stone of death and rebirth, she was, with a strange wisdom that drew her physically to any article made of precious iron. She was called lodestone, and I have been told that even the great Black Stone from the stars could call her to its side and hold her as tightly as a mother holds her child. The fourth of my amulets was the eye stone, round and glowing gold like the all-seeing Goddess-eye of the moon in heaven's air. A brilliant eye-spot in its center stood for the eye of the spirit that brings light in darkness. I needed its power now.

I prayed: "O Mother, send away the ghost of this Greek, whose people dare to despise You and worship Your sons, the wrangling jealous gods, sanctioning their crimes against women. I am Your daughter, a warrior in Your service. The Greek died trying to steal land and flocks from Your faithful children. Cast him into the deepest pit of forgetfulness, Mother, and give me a purificatory vision. I am at rest in Your dear body."

I sat, holding my amulets. The hours passed. I allowed myself to sink deeply into the soft dark, making no attempt to control my thoughts but allowing them to wander at will. Sometimes I spoke aloud; but the dead sound of my voice in that muffled chamber was disturbing, so I fell silent. I wavered in and out of a trance state. I remember several times crawling over to the water cup and the waste hole. I slept and awoke, but after a while I hardly knew when I was awake and when I was dreaming.

I thought often of my home farm, with my dear mother presiding over the hearth, and of my three elder sisters with their husbands and their children. I had two brothers also, but they, of course, had gone to live in the homes of their wives, to become members of another maternal clan. My mother's own elder sister, Leukippe, had never married and still lived with us. She was our resident Crone, a holy woman, the aunt who knew everything. She had been a priestess. She understood the arts of healing and the lore of herbs and stones. She spoke often to the Goddess. It was Aunt Leukippe who sewed up my wounds after a battle and bathed them in healing potions. It was Aunt Leukippe who told us the stories of the stars when we were little children, and taught us the sagas of the foremothers, and led us in singing their songs. As my mother's sister, she was almost as dear to me as my own bloodmother. Aunt Leukippe was my alma mater—my mother-of-the-soul. In the times when I feared that I would never be able to kill a Greek and thus would have to remain unmarried, I longed to dedicate my life to the Goddess and become an Aunt Leukippe to the children of my sisters, devoting my later years to studying and teaching.

But now things had changed. Having achieved my kill and thus demonstrated an inheritable power over the enemies of my people, I could allow myself to bear children of my own. I thought about my male lovers. Even at my advanced age, I had had only three of them. Training as a warrior left one little time for dalliance. I would not choose any of those three, I thought, to serve as my child-begetter. No, I would have to find a man better qualified, a man with a more fatherly temperament and perhaps some useful, teachable skills. A smith might do well. Smiths were seers, wizards, and highly respected craftsmen among my people. They were considered so valuable that sometimes the Council of Mothers deliberately had them lamed so that they would not run away and join other tribes. The ritual dance of the smiths was known as the limping dance, because all the smiths affected a left-footed limp whether they were physically lamed or not. In this way, they honored their tutelary craft god, Velchanos, the lame deity whose forges lay under the fire mountains. His spirit was sometimes manifested above these mountains as a pillar of fire by night and a pillar of dark cloud by day. Our tradition said that the Goddess Herself had loved Velchanos as Her favorite son, had lamed him, and had sent him down to the underworld to forge the lightnings and rule all the smiths.

From time to time I brought my thoughts back to my present situation, reminding myself that these wanderings were trivial and that I should be thinking in a more focused way. I tried to concentrate on higher matters or to keep my mind empty and open to a possible vision. I craved a vision. I hoped that the Mother would honor me with a truly transcendent experience. Perhaps that was hubris, but I was ready to be taken out of myself.

No preparation in this world, however, could have made me ready for what actually happened.

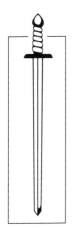

CHAPTER 3

I MUST HAVE FALLEN INTO AN UNCONSCIOUS TRANCE. I know there was a dark space, in which I was dimly aware of something like a sense of movement. I thought afterward that I had seemed to be traveling through an infinite void. There was no progress to this travel. It went from nowhere to nowhere.

▼ ▼ ▼

I awoke suddenly in a place so evil that at first I thought myself in one of the more unpleasant backwaters of Hades. The womb chamber and the warmth that I had generated within it were gone. Chilly in my nakedness, I lay on a bank of grass in the open air—but such air! It stank, with a stale, stuffy, alien odor that was like nothing I had ever smelled before. It masked all the scents of grass, leaves, water, animals, and other environmental smells that I was used to. This nasty air was the characteristic atmosphere of the strange world in which I found myself. I found it impossible to draw a single truly refreshing breath.

It was nighttime. The sky was dark, but like the foul air it was alien to my experience, not a true dark night, but a muddy, rusty, dull glow that obscured most of the stars. I gazed up through this sulfurous murk, seeking the familiar constellations. I was able to find the seven bright stars that we call the Seven Sisters, in the constellation of Artemis Kalliste, the Bear-Mother, and from there I located the still point of the heavens in the constellation of the Bear-Child. That, I knew, was north. As I searched for other bright stars to help me locate the mostly hidden constellations, I saw what I thought must be a flying demon: a pair of stars close together, like eyes, moving across the sky with slow deliberation, not quickly like stars that suddenly fall and wink out. Then I saw another demon, and another. They were crisscrossing the sky in several directions. The leaden veil of sour air seemed to be thick enough to hold them up among the stars.

To my horror, I next saw two similar demon eyes approaching me on the ground. The brilliant lights were coming through the dull darkness faster than any horse could run, accompanied by a hissing roar that I took to be the demon's voice. Despite my training, I felt a terrible fear. Was I to meet an ignominious end here, in this grotesque place, being devoured by some dragon-like creature? Shakily I drew my sword and resolved to die wielding it, as a warrior should; but my heart sank at the fierce, irresistible rush of the adversary's approach. Surely it came more swiftly than an eagle swooping out of the sky upon its prey! I stood, trembling, sword in hand. To my astonishment, the bright-eyed monster passed me by, throwing long white beams from its blazing eyes as it passed. I had just time to see a dark, humped shape, like a huge turtle. Then it was departing. To my further astonishment, I saw two more eyes on its rear. These eyes were an unbelievable glowing red—a more luminous red than the color of the sun as it sinks into the Western Gate at day's end.

Then a similar object approached from the other direction and passed by me just as the first had. Another came, and another. Always they kept to the broad, flat path that I now saw running beside my bank of grass. They were not alive, after all. I saw that they ran on wheels, not feet. They were wagons of some kind, but no animal drew them. No animal could draw any vehicle at such speeds. I had almost grown used to their passing when, with another shock, I saw an enormous one coming with a roar like a hundred charging lions. This one was higher than a house and as long as two houses. The sight of it gave me another quiver of fear, but it passed by like all the others, keeping to the same unnaturally flat path.

The eastern sky was turning a dirty pale gray now. I understood that dawn was near. As the light grew, I was able to make out more details in my surroundings. Beside the flat path ran a line of very tall, straight, limbless and leafless tree trunks, placed far apart but joined at their tops by a number of long black ropes hanging from curious crosspieces. Down the center of the flat path ran a band of chalk-white pigment, perhaps as wide as one hand's span. I noticed that the speeding wagon-things coming from my left kept to the near side of this white band, while those coming from my right kept to the far side. Thus they never interfered with each other in their dizzying rush. It was like a bizarre copy of a custom of my own people — that of walking to the right on a roadway, to keep the left heart-hand free to touch passersby in friendly greeting.

All too soon, however, I was to discover that the wagon-things were occupied by real human beings and that some of these human beings were anything but friendly.

One of the vehicles stopped suddenly, with a curious screaming sound, right in front of me. A young man poked his head out of a hole in its side and spoke to me. "Hey, baby, ain't-chu cold? C'mere, we'll warm you up!" Then he gave a nasty laugh, which was echoed by other men inside the vehicle.

I shifted my mind into the thought-sensitive state that Aunt Leukippe had taught me, trying to understand the meaning behind their language, which was like none that I had ever heard. Usually, the thought-sensitive state allowed people to communicate without being able to speak each other's tongue. It was a useful skill for merchants who traveled to many foreign places and for priestesses who listened to many dialects. Alas, I wished that I had paid more attention to Aunt Leukippe's lessons. My skill was imperfect. I could pick up only a portion of the men's intent as they talked among themselves. One thing only I understood very well: their attitude toward me was decidedly hostile.

"What's she doin' out here in the middle of nuthin'?" one of them said.

"Who the hell knows? She must be some kind of nut-case streaker."

"Bet she does a lot of runnin'. Just look at that bod."

"Yeah, look at that fuckin' big pigsticker she's got, too. You wanna mess with that?"

"Aw, come on, you guys. There's only one of her. Four against one. You wanna pass up a golden opportunity?"

"Hey, Bobby. Can'tchu never give it a rest?"

"Whaddaya mean? How often do you see meat like that hangin' on the roadside? You guys crazy or what? C'mon, chickens. Grow up and get some cocks."

The first man now opened a larger hole in the wagon and emerged, walking slowly toward me. Three others followed him. They were odd-looking men indeed, wearing odd-looking garments. Though they were young, their bare arms looked flabby and wasted, like the arms of old men or of men who had never performed normal physical tasks. Their bellies were round and soft. I could see from their gait that they were not fit or strong. Therefore, even though they outnumbered me, I thought I might win if I had to fight them. I had a weapon, and they had none that I could see.

"C'mere, honey," said the one called Bobby. "Don't give us no trouble and we won't hurt you. We just wanna have a little

18

fun, OK?" His eyes were cruel, cold, and contemptuous. I gripped my sword tightly and stood my ground.

"Beware of me," I said. "I am a trained warrior in the service of the Mother. You will rape me only at the price of your own blood." Sensing their hatred of women, I thought they might be Greeks. I spoke in the Hellenic tongue.

"She's some kinda foreigner. No spik da English."

"What kinda talk is that?"

"Dunno. Sounds like Greek to me."

"Let's rush her if we're gonna do it, stick her in the car and take off. All this open space is makin' me nervous. Traffic goin' by and all."

"There ain't no traffic," said Bobby. "D'you see any traffic? Look, she'll understand this, all right." From some recess in his garments, he drew a small, brightly polished dagger, which he waved threateningly at me. "Put down the pigsticker, honey," he said. "We don't want no bad stuff here. Everything nice and friendly, OK?"

I almost laughed at his foolishness. A silly little knife against a sword in the hand of a trained Maiden of the Mother! He was not even clever enough to keep from signaling his rush, a fraction of a second before he leapt at me. I was ready. My sword flicked out, and his absurd dagger went spinning away into the grass, followed by the first three fingers of his right hand, followed in turn by a jet of blood. Bobby screamed like a dying rabbit.

"Jesus Christ, the bitch cut my fuckin' hand off!" he yelled. "Shoot her, Joe! Waste her! Get me to a goddamn doctor!"

"Let's get the hell out of here," another one said.

They started to back away, with Bobby clutching his hand and whimpering. I stepped deliberately toward them, prepared to strike again.

The one called Joe pulled out a short stick of some black metal and pointed it at me, saying, "Stop right there, bitch."

This stick looked even less like a useful weapon than Bobby's child-size knife. Seeing them waver, I seized the advantage, gave my battle cry, and sprang at them. There was a sound like a sudden thunderclap. Something searingly hot bit into my thigh, and I fell. My sword was jarred from my hand. Now, I thought, I am helpless. They will charge and pin me down. To my surprise, they did not. They were running as if a whole company of warriors might be chasing them. They tumbled into their strange vehicle. With a piercing, shrieking sound, it rushed away.

I tried to stand up and could not. There was a hole in my thigh, bleeding vigorously, causing considerable pain. By what evil magic could I have been thus wounded, when no blade had touched me? Fortunately for me, these peculiar men seemed lacking in the determination to match their hostility. I decided that they could not have been Greeks; even with all their faults, the Greeks were not so cowardly as to run away from one wounded warrior.

I lay in the grass, trying to gather sufficient calm to assess my situation. My pain was increased by the shock of so much strangeness, the bad air, the ugly sky, the demonic vehicles, the mindless hostility of the only other human beings I had seen. I must have become unconscious for a while. When I awoke, the sun was up.

Now there were a great many of the strange vehicles rushing by on the roadway. There were more of the huge houselike ones that roared so terrifyingly. They bore brilliant colors on their sides, formed into evocative symbols. I thought that if each vehicle carried hostile men, then indeed I faced an overwhelming army. I must find a place to hide and protect myself.

I tried to rise and fell again, crying out with the pain in my leg. How could I have been so injured by the empty air? This was fearful magic. I was weak from loss of blood. I staggered and floundered helplessly. I began to crawl away from the side of the road, leaving a trail of blood in the grass.

Dimly I saw that another vehicle had stopped in the same spot as the first. Were the men coming back to finish me? Or was it a fresh group, with better weapon skill? I struggled to my knees and seized my sword, though my arm was shaking with weakness. I determined to die as a warrior should, blade in hand, facing the enemy and not permitting my fear to show in my eyes.

This time, a single woman came from the vehicle. She was dressed like the men, but she was older in years, tall, with a thickish body and a cronemother's graying hair. I sensed no hostility from her, so I bent my head politely in reverence for her cronehood. She spoke to me gently, asking questions that I could almost understand when I made a painful effort at concentration.

"What's the matter with you? Where are your clothes? Why are you here? Are you hurt?"

I couldn't catch any comprehensible images, but her facial expression and tone of voice alone conveyed friendly concern. With a rush of gratitude, I sensed the woman's sympathy and willingness to help. Hers was the first kindly face I had seen in this terrible place. I began to weep with relief. I sheathed my sword and held out my hands to her. She helped me to my feet. She drew my arm over her shoulders and half carried me down the slope toward her vehicle.

Seeing that she intended to put me into the vehicle, I drew back. What might be the destination of this dreadful horseless chariot? Could the woman be a decoy, sent to betray me by a false show of kindness? If so, she was very skillful. I could sense no duplicity in her mind.

She urged and comforted me. "It's all right," she said. "Don't be afraid. Whatever happened to you, it won't happen again. I'm going to take care of you."

She spoke the same bizarre language as the men, yet her inner meanings revealed only goodwill. It was a strain for me,

21

trying to hold the thought-sensitive state through pain and weakness. I knew that I must concentrate. Perhaps my life would depend on the correct reading of this woman's intentions.

She leaned me up against the mirror-smooth metal of her vehicle, opened a door in it, and pulled out a strange garment like a cloak with sleeves. "Here, put this on," she said, laying it over my shoulders. She drew my arms through the sleeves and fastened the garment in front. She reached into the vehicle again and brought forth a length of cloth, amazingly soft, dyed in fantastic colors and intricate patterns. Never had I seen such a cloth. I thought surely it had been spun by the Goddess Herself.

The woman bound this cloth tightly around my wounded thigh. My seeping blood stained and spoiled the beautiful colors. More than any other gesture, her sacrifice of this elegant thing convinced me of her sincerity.

I allowed her to seat me inside the vehicle and even to fasten a kind of strap across my chest, although this apparent binding made me uneasy. She took a seat beside me and pulled a similar strap across her own body.

"Where to?" she asked. "Do you want to go home, or to the hospital, or to your own doctor? Where do you live?"

I said, "I am a stranger in this place. I came from Themiskyra."

The woman seemed surprised. "So you don't speak English," she said. *"Parlez-vous français? Sprechen Sie Deutsch? ¿Habla usted español?"*

I realized that she was trying other languages on me, but none of the words sounded even remotely familiar. I answered in Greek, the only foreign language that I knew. She shook her head. She resorted to gesture. She put her hand on her chest, saying, "Diana." Then she put her hand on my chest with an inquiring look. I understood that she was asking my name. I said, "Antiope." I was pleased to hear that her name was like one

22

belonging to the Great Goddess: Dione. Perhaps she was a priestess.

"Well, Ann," she said, "it's clear that you need a translator as well as medical care. But that leg will have to be seen to right away. I'll take you to the emergency room at the hospital."

As she spoke these words, a truly terrifying image flashed through my mind. I saw a vast cave, filled with an unnatural blue-white brilliance. Crowds of people in white clothes were doing unnatural things to other people, who were choking, screaming, moaning, or writhing in pain. Some lay still, like corpses. There was blood everywhere. In the frenetic activity, hideous devices like torture machines were applied to parts of the victims' bodies. When they sank into deathlike immobility, they were taken away to an unimaginable destination where, I thought, they would suffer even more.

I groaned in horrified protest. Diana turned to look at me. "What? No? No hospital?"

I recognized a negative word. "N-n-no," I gasped. "No. No!" I swung my hand up before my face, palm out, to signify desperate rejection.

"All right, calm down. No hospital. You seem to understand that word at least. I must say you've got me very curious. It's not every day I find a pretty young woman on the roadside, wearing nothing but a little leather bag and an odd-looking old sword, speaking no English, and bleeding from a hole in her leg. There's a dandy story in you, and I'd like to know it. So we'll go to my place. I can get you taken care of there. We'll go to Diana's house for a little while, OK?"

I gazed into her eyes, trying to fathom her intentions. I felt that I was missing the nuances of her speech. Her expression still seemed guilelessly friendly. Taking my earnest look for assent, she patted my unhurt knee and did something to start her vehicle. Thus began one of the most remarkable and memorable experiences of my life: my very first ride in a car.

I thought later that my dizziness and pain helped to distract me from the worst terrors of this experience. Had I been able to give it full attention, I might have gone out of my mind. I had never dreamed that any vehicle could move so fast. Vegetation along the roadside flashed by in a blur of green. Diana's car followed, passed, or dodged around others at a horrifying rate, but never struck anything and never left the roadway. At first I covered my eyes and waited for a crashing impact, but the car kept going. I began to trust Diana's control of her impossible vehicle and to open my eyes to the alien world around me.

When we came to the town, I was astonished by the diverse shapes and brilliant colors of buildings and other structures. There were gigantic pictures set up along the road for travelers to see and enjoy. Sometimes the pictures showed human beings many times life size, painted in colors of amazing vibrancy. Sometimes posts at the roadside bore strange designs in shiny black, snow white, blood red, and dandelion yellow, outshining the brightest flowers.

At first I took the houses for palaces or temples. They were so splendid and so colorful. Some were as tall as great trees. Others spread out low to the ground, with almost as many chambers as a small village. In my innocence, I imagined that whole tribes must live together in such places. I thought perhaps the entire town might be a fantastic necropolis of tomb shrines, chapels, and sacred attendants for honoring the foremothers, because at first it did not seem to be a living town. There were very few people to be seen among the splendid dwellings. I saw no children, goats, dogs, chickens, cattle, pigs, doves, donkeys, or horses; no signs of people at work; no one weaving, pounding grain, building boats, sharpening tools, hoeing vegetable gardens. I saw no fields of growing crops, no cooking fires, no persons carrying burdens of any kind. There was no evidence of daily living, as I and my people understood it. For all their flower-bright colors and astonishing shapes, the houses seemed dead.

In the center of the town, however, there were even bigger buildings and great throngs of people in wildly colorful clothes, walking about in every direction. I thought it must be a festival day. The people had dressed in their finest garments and gathered together to celebrate the Goddess. But then, who was taking care of the flocks and herds, and where were they?

Diana guided her vehicle to one of the quiet houses and stopped. The walls of this house were as white as new-fallen snow. The door was shocking red, a fresh blood color. The roof was black. Maiden, Mother, and Crone colors. Surely, I thought, Diana must be a holy woman. My impression was confirmed when a huge door, large enough to admit the entire car, suddenly opened by itself and allowed us to enter. This woman could control even the very walls!

Diana helped me out of the car and half carried me into the amazing chambers of her house. My vision was growing dim, yet I felt fresh astonishment at the rooms, which were more light and airy than any rooms I had ever seen. Window spaces were covered by a thin, perfectly transparent substance. The walls were as flat as water in a bowl and alive with color. Everywhere, even on the floors, there were rich fabrics worth a queen's ransom.

Diana laid me on a bed as soft as the finest goose down. She covered me with a vast skin that felt like fur but was not fur. Then she picked up a small violet-colored object from the bedside stand, held it to her head, and spoke to it, as if it were alive. Though my mind was fading in and out, I made intense efforts to concentrate on her speech.

"Come on, Jeff, you owe me one," she was saying. "You know I wouldn't insist if it weren't an emergency. As a matter of fact, I think she's passing out right now. No, it has to be here. I have my reasons." She paused, then said, "Thanks, Jeff. I'll be waiting."

Overcome by stresses of body and mind, I allowed the softness of the bed to lull me to sleep. Later, I awoke suddenly to a fresh bout of pain. I found myself once more uncovered. A young man was bending over me, probing my wound.

My first thought was that Diana had indeed betrayed me into the hands of hostile men. I jumped and struggled. Diana and the man held my shoulders down, while she spoke soothingly to me.

"Ann, be still. He's here to help you. He's a doctor. This is Jeff, my nephew. Please don't be afraid." My wound was bleeding again, and I felt weaker than ever. I sank back on the pillows. Diana petted me and smoothed the hair back from my forehead, murmuring quietly. Still, I watched the young man as if I were a trapped animal and he the trapper.

I couldn't understand Diana's use of the word *doctor*. The image in her mind seemed to mean a healer. But how could a man be a healer? Men have no life magic. Yet his hands were almost as gentle as a woman's. He seemed to know what he was doing.

I saw that the skin around the wound was red and puffy, so I knew that it was already inflamed and that the cleaning of it would hurt. As Aunt Leukippe had taught me to do when she had ministered to my battle wounds, I centered my mind to withstand the pain.

The man Jeff did not begin by cleaning the wound. Instead, he took a thin silvery vessel from a leather bag. He filled the vessel with a clear water. Then he pricked my leg in several places with the vessel's tiny tooth, as thin as a silken thread. It felt like the sting of a very small bee. In a short time, all my pain faded away as if it had never been. My leg lost all feeling, as if it were someone else's leg, not mine. The male healer cleaned, sewed, and bandaged the wound under my very eyes without causing any pain at all. A miracle! Such healing magic my people could never even have imagined!

While he worked, Jeff talked to Diana. He criticized Aunt Leukippe's healing techniques. "Where could she have gotten such scars, Aunt Di?" he asked. "Look here at this, and this. Looks like somebody sewed her up with butcher's twine. Furthermore, the girl's a real fitness freak; she has muscles like rocks. What is she, your personal wolf-child from the north woods?"

Diana only smiled and lifted her shoulders.

"Yeah, I know," he went on. "You smell a story, right? Well, I'll give you an item to think about. This is a bullet wound. I'll have to report it."

"Don't, Jeff. Let this one go. For me."

"I could get in trouble."

"I'll never tell. And she can't."

"Are you going to keep her here, like some stray kitten? She must have a home somewhere. A family. People who will be looking for her. You should at least find out what language she speaks."

"I will," Diana said, "when she's better. Right now she's my responsibility and your patient. You just concentrate on fixing her up. Later, we'll sort out the rest."

Tears spilled from my eyes. I understood Jeff's images of *home* and *family*, the universal images of comfort. Would I ever see my home and family again? Here I was in the most alien place anyone could imagine, at the mercy of strangers who could not understand my words, in a land so utterly bizarre that I could not tell its evil magic from its good magic. I could not even guess in which direction to travel to return to my home. I covered my face and wept.

"Is she in pain?" Diana asked.

"Not yet," Jeff said. "I'll give her a sedative. See that she takes one of these antibiotics every four hours when she's awake. I'll stop by tomorrow and have another look at her."

"I appreciate this, Jeff."

"Anything for my favorite aunt." He leaned over and kissed Diana's cheek. Then he stung me again with his tiny water vessel, this time in my buttock. He closed his leather bag and went away. I thought my inner spirit was too agonized, too much in turmoil, to make sleep possible, but I was wrong. Despite my general sense of desolation, I soon lapsed into a dreamless darkness.

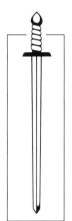

CHAPTER 4

WEEKS PASSED WHILE MY WOUND HEALED. I LIVED WITH Diana and began to learn her language, practicing my thought-sensitive state more assiduously than ever before in my life. Little by little, I also learned how to live and move in that house of miracles. Never in my wildest fantasies could I have imagined such a place of wonders.

At first I believed that Diana must be the greatest priestess in her land. She owned things so magical that not even the queens of Skythia could have dreamed of them. The most favored oracles of the Mother had never mentioned even the possibility of such things. Yet Diana presided like the highest of high priestesses over fabulous things and even seemed to think them commonplace.

There were the lamps, burning steadily with their brilliant light at any time during the day or night, for as long as light was wanted. They would flick on or off at a mere touch. It was never necessary to obtain oil for them or to keep a fire going for their wicks. Their light was not firelight at all but something like the brilliance of tiny suns.

There were places where hidden waters gushed forth at the turn of a handle. There were not only cold waters but also heated waters, always ready. There were no boiling stones to heat, no fires to build. Diana never built a fire, not even for cooking. She cooked her food in a magic box that could be made very hot, either inside or on top. I touched it once and blistered my finger, even though there were no flames to be seen.

Another magic box was always cold inside, to keep food fresh. It was strange food, the like of which I had never seen. There were endless varieties of meats, cheeses, and cereals. Diana ate meat *every day*, as if each day of the year were a feast day.

I never saw Diana hunt, fish, or take harvest from the earth. Food came out of boxes that she brought home in her car.

All necessities were contained inside the house, even the latrine places, which were perfectly clean, odorless stools hollowed and filled with a clear water that could be changed after every evacuation. Even that water was good enough to drink. Although there was no running stream for bathing, one could stand in a large tub and let water run over the body from what I learned to call a shower. Alternatively, one could fill the tub with warmed water and lie down in it. One could bathe every day.

Diana and everything in her house were kept unbelievably clean. There were no insects inside the walls. No rain or mud ever got in. The hard transparent panels in the windows, which I learned to call glass, let in light but kept out every drop of rainwater. These glass panels could be opened and closed. No flying insects could get in even when they were open, because every opening was protected by a fabric of close-woven metal threads.

There were many magic boxes. Some, called radios, contained music and human voices. The sounds were always there, any time of the day or night, to be heard at the twist of a knob. Other boxes contained music, voices, and pictures so realistic that the box seemed filled with an infinite, ever-changing variety of tiny people and scenes. Diana called this television, teevy, the tube, or the box. I soon found that I couldn't study language from television. My gift of tongues couldn't understand the people in the box unless I knew their words already. I couldn't hear thought-meanings unless I was in the real presence of the speakers.

As I began to acquire the vocabulary of her language, Diana was more and more surprised. Mother Mnemosyne had always favored me with the Muses' gift. Once I heard a word, I rarely forgot it. Diana found this amazing. "Just imagine, at first I thought you were feebleminded," she would say. "Ann, you're a ruddy genius. How can you remember like that?"

I would smile and shrug. I enjoyed her praise. I didn't want to admit that this oceanic inpouring of new words, together with a thousand alien experiences and concepts all at once, strained almost to the breaking point my ability to absorb them. At night I would lie awake for hours, running the new word lists over and over in my mind like a saga priestess learning the oral traditions. Sometimes I wondered if it was for this kind of learning that my gift had been given me in the first place.

It was hard for me to sort out the pronouns. I called myself *you* and Diana *I*, as she did, until she corrected me. I couldn't easily grasp the distinction. In my language, all members of the same clan could be called by the same word referring to their joint mother-blood. Diana had he-pronouns and she-pronouns. No androgynous beings were allowed in this world. When an individual's sex was in doubt or not ascertainable, as in the case of an animal or a person spoken of generally, somehow it was always a *he* rather than a *she*, as in my own mother tongue. It was hard to know, too, when to use *we* and *they*. This language made many more separations and barriers between members of the same race than I was used to noticing.

While I was learning, Diana kept trying to discover where I had come from and how I had come to be lying wounded in the grass where she found me. She believed that I had a forgetting disease, called amnesia. I tried to satisfy her curiosity. Combining mime with my still-scanty vocabulary, I explained about the men who had threatened me and shot me when I scared them away. "Bastards," Diana said. I was puzzled by this word, which seemed to be an insult yet was also related to a lack of parentage.

"Bastards—what meaning?" I asked.

"It's an impolite word, like a curse, for somebody born out of wedlock—somebody whose parents weren't married at the time when he was born."

"Married?" The image in her mind was something like the custom of the Greeks, whose gods allowed them to enslave women and lock them up in man-owned houses. "Bastards escape from married?"

She laughed. "In a way, I guess. People are called legitimate if their mother and father were lawfully married to each other, and illegitimate, or bastards, if not. It's supposed to be a bad thing to be illegitimate."

"How you know men's mother-father not married?"

"I don't know. It's just a conventional crude term for somebody who acts bad."

"Why bad to escape married?"

She smiled somewhat ruefully. "I guess it's not bad when you put it that way. It was only three years ago that I escaped a bad marriage—seems like an eternity. But that's divorce, a whole different thing. Nothing to do with the state of bastardy. The problem with that is that a bastard doesn't have any legal right of inheritance or any legal claim on the father's property."

"Men own property?"

"Usually men own more than women do, or they have more money to get property. This is a patriarchal society, Ann. The men mostly control it."

Behind these words I saw her mind's picture of whole nations given over to the glorification of men at women's expense, to the subordination of mothers and female creators, and to the exaltation of men's jealousy and violence beyond all balance or reason. Diana's people seemed even worse than the Greeks.

Diana corrected my impression that the four men I had met were national enemies. She said they were members of the same nation. Many men in her nation attacked or raped women whenever they could. She explained that women had to be on guard against men all the time.

"Then why women have not weapons?" I asked, shaking my sword.

"It wouldn't do much good," she said sadly. "Men can always have the same weapons and often can use them better."

"Tchah. Men cowards," I said, remembering how they had run from me.

"Not all of them," Diana said. "Not all are cruel or bad, either. Only some are."

"One is too many," I said. "In my home, raper man be killed."

"I sure wish I could find your home, Ann," she said. "Where could it be?"

Sometimes she set before me a multicolored globe, saying that it represented our Mother Earth. She asked me to point to my country. This was one of her nonsense things. As if a painted ball could stand for the Mother, the rocks, the soil, the caves and deep places, the floors of the seas, the womb at Themiskyra! I would laugh and spin the colored ball to show that I appreciated her joke. Then she showed me colored maps in books made of thin dry stuff called paper. These were supposed to show the earth's surface, but they were all crazy colors that never appear on the land. Diana often joked in this way. She seemed to think she could find my home by such jokes.

I told her about my home, as much as I could verbalize. She said she had never heard of such a place. She couldn't understand the motherclan or the sisterhood. She had no concept even of Her, the Great One.

"Mother of mothers," I would explain, spreading out my arms to indicate the whole universe. "World birth mother. Sky, air, water, soil, fire, stars, moon. Animals. People. All."

"I guess you mean God," Diana said. I saw in her mind an image of a male divinity. I shook my head vigorously, as I had learned to indicate the negative.

"No god," I said. "God smaller, you understand? Mother's — uh — friend, helper, also child. God no birth giver. Man no power for that."

"Well, men don't say God gave birth to the world. They say God made the world."

"Hah. Only power of men. Make things, magic things but not alive. Only Mother makes alive."

"That makes sense," Diana said. "But I don't know much about theology. Some day you can discuss it with somebody more knowledgeable."

I understood that she wasn't really serious about her male god, but she knew no alternatives. The women of her world were spiritually impoverished by almost total ignorance of their own Goddess. I wondered how this could have happened, but I turned my attention to other matters for the time being.

Every moment I spent with Diana was an intense teaching-learning session. Limping about the house, I helped her cook and clean while we talked and pantomimed incessantly. After dark, when other people wouldn't see me, we went outdoors. I learned about the trees, the flowers in her garden, the insects. It was a relief to me to be able to dig my fingers into soil, to touch the rocks of my Mother's bones once more, to see what few stars the strange pale-colored sky could show.

Sometimes Diana left me alone and spent many hours at a time away from home, "on assignment," as she called it. At other times she shut herself in her "den" and worked on a wonderful word-making machine called a typewriter. This machine

34

made alphabet letters on paper that was like the pages of Diana's books. These letters showed words to the eye. Long ago I had heard of certain holy scribes in the temples at Themiskyra and elsewhere who commanded a similar magic of letters. I thought it would be a great skill to learn. I thought Diana must be a sacred person to have such a skill, but she told me that writing and reading were not considered unusual in her world. She said almost everyone could understand word-reading, and in time she would teach me that too. She had developed an almost boundless faith in my learning ability.

Diana often asked me to name things in my own language. She pointed to this or that, then to me. I would say the word, sometimes two or three times over, then she would write it. There were many objects that I had no word for because such things did not exist in my motherland. When she asked for such a word, I would simply put my finger on my lips and shake my head.

One day Diana produced a small box and asked me to speak into it in my own language. I did so, at some length. Then she pressed buttons, and I was disturbed to hear my own voice speaking back out of the box. I thought it must be a soul-catcher. "Antiope not in box!" I cried, reaching for it angrily.

Diana caught my hands and soothed me. "It's all right," she said. "I'm going to try to find your home with this. I'll take it to some people who know many languages. They'll listen, and maybe find out what your language is."

"People not make evil on my voice?" I asked apprehensively.

"No, Ann. No evil. Trust me."

I did trust her. Gradually we became good companions, almost like sisters. Diana said she was neglecting her work sometimes because she was fascinated by the task of teaching me. She said the gaps in my knowledge were extremely mysterious. It was almost as if I had literally been born yesterday, although I was full grown. At the same time, I noticed many gaps in her knowledge of some of the most basic things. I thought someday I could repay all her kindness by teaching her.

In the end, my mother tongue turned out to be one of the unknown things. Diana said a learned man had listened to my voice on the box and tentatively identified the language as a very archaic or very corrupt Greek, whatever that meant. He couldn't be sure of anything except that it was no living language. No one had ever heard it spoken before. That made me feel lonely indeed. My country was so far away that no one could even guess where it might be.

I suffered from my loneliness, though I hid this from Diana. I didn't want to seem ungrateful for her kindness. Still, it was a lonely life. Diana slept alone in her bed, and I slept in her "spare room," either on the bed or on the floor, which sometimes felt better to me. She seemed never to want the comfortable touch of another body, even though her bed was large enough for three or four sleepers together. She lived alone in her huge magical house, which could easily have accommodated two large clans.

I found this self-imposed loneliness in daily living hard to understand. It wasn't that I was unable to live in loneliness. At home on several occasions I had gone alone into the mountains to fast and meditate, to invite envoys of the Mother to communicate with me. I was accustomed to living for weeks at a time without seeing another human being. But then I could return to the warmth of my mother-house, to my sisters and their children: their stroking hands, their skin warmth, the scent of their bodies, and the reassurance of their presence.

Diana seemed to accept aloneness as the basic condition of living. I thought this might have something to do with the lack of Mother spirit in her world, but I didn't know how to speak of this. It was hard for me to live so untouched, but I tried to adjust to it, on the theory that this must be what the Mother intended for me.

As far as I could tell, Diana lived a celibate life. She slept alone always, never inviting a man to her bed. Because of this, I assumed that she preferred women. Therefore, as an expression of my gratitude and love for her, I offered myself to her. One evening when she had retired early, I limped naked into her bedroom. She was lying in bed with her broad glass eyes propped across her face, a book of printed letters before her.

I sat down on the bed and began to caress her body in invitation, as some of my sisters had taught me long ago. To my astonishment, she recoiled with a horrified expression, crying, "Ann, what are you doing?"

"I will do love with you," I said. "I see you lonely. You have no men, but sometimes women are better. I know how to make joy, man or woman."

"No!" she exclaimed, startling me so much that I drew away, puzzled and a little hurt.

"I don't mean to upset you, Ann," she said in a softer tone. "But I'm not like that. I mean, I don't make love to women."

Now I was astonished again. "Never in life?" I asked. "Not in young girl time even?"

"Never," she said. "We—my people—believe in sticking to one sex or the other. And many of us think making love to others of the same sex is not natural."

"Is natural," I said. "Even for animals, all children, also adults sometimes. Love makes different feelings for different sexes, but is the same Mother's gift for all. How can you turn away half the Mother's gift?"

Diana shook her head. "I don't know about the ways of your Mother, my dear. Perhaps you're right, but you see I can't do it. I'm too old to retrain my sexual tastes."

"I can teach," I said. "In my homeland, wise women teach all girls. Feel very good."

"It wouldn't work," Diana sighed. "I can't relate to a woman that way. I have had only men. That's what I'm used to."

"But you have no men now. Men not come here. Where are men for you?"

"Nowhere at present," she said. "Since my divorce I've been chaste. Men aren't interested in a gray-haired old woman like me."

"Your men are stupid," I said. "Old women better, more practice."

"Perhaps. But we don't think that way in this country. I don't want a man very much, anyway. At my age the impulses are easily ignored. I'm too busy to bother about love affairs."

Looking into her mind through these speeches and later conversations, I found in her a surprising cloud of confusion and even ignorance about sexuality in general. Not only was she unaware of the female-to-female dimension but even her experience of men was small. She had known only a few in addition to her former husband, and while married to him, she had taken no other lovers. That was what her society considered normal! It seemed that the least possible sexual experience was the norm for Diana's people. Conversely, they often accepted without excessive protest what seemed to me a hideous abnormality, the crime of rape, which was nearly unthinkable among us, except for what we heard of the evil ways of the Greeks.

Diana's people considered violent rape a crime, true, but according to Diana the criminals frequently escaped with slight punishment, even if their victims were injured. Rape without injury—that is, sexual contact that a woman did not want—could go altogether unpunished.

I was especially angry about this when I remembered the vicious, witless men who had injured me even though there had been no war between us. I told Diana about the punishment decreed by the Mother for a man who raped. He was to have all his genitals sliced off, preferably by his victim. Then he was left alone to pour out the blood that was his own mother's gift of his

38

life, because in offering an offense to women, he would have dishonored his mother and no longer deserved her gift. If he survived, he would be an outcast from the motherclan and a landless, homeless laborer for anyone who might consent to feed him. Never in anyone's living memory had any man of my tribe committed the sin meriting such a punishment. Diana smiled at this, and said that the Mother's law might provide the only truly useful deterrent.

As I learned Diana's language and began to understand the speeches from the teevy box, I found myself exposed to daily pictures of a highly bizarre culture. I often saw images of men doing violence to women and to each other for no apparent reason. Diana said the people in the box were only pretending, not really hurting one another. Sometimes I could see that they struck without actually connecting. Most of the time, however, their battles looked genuine. Furthermore, even though the teevy violence was faked, Diana said that great numbers of people believed in it and even modeled their own lives after this irrational hostility.

Conversely, the teevy box almost never showed people pleasuring one another. There were no stroking or massaging and no real sex, although young women and men were often shown eating each other's mouths. There was nothing to instruct mothers about massaging their babies, or nursing, or doing midwifery. There were no old wise women in the teevy box. A few elder women appeared occasionally, either to be laughed at or to be shown as evil persons. Their faces were painted with strange bright colors just like the faces of younger women. None of the women looked real.

It was a peculiar society indeed: filled with miracles of comfort in the home, while everyone lived in anxiety and discomfort of the spirit, afraid to be close in the human way, afraid of their sexual nature, afraid of their own compatriots. I was to find these first impressions hugely confirmed as time went on, when I discovered even more about the incredible world to which the Mother had seen fit to send me.

Having no other person with whom to share my sexual urges, I followed the usual custom of my clansisters and pleasured myself by means of my omphalos — the small Goddess pillar at the temple gate of my body, where women best feel the heavenly bliss of the Mother. I did this once on an evening when Diana and I were sitting quietly together before the teevy box. She looked at me oddly as I exposed my loins and began to touch my holy spot. Although I was preoccupied with my pleasure, I noticed in a peripheral sort of way that she was fidgeting uncomfortably as I approached my climax. When I finally relaxed with a few little sweet cries and a long sigh or two, I smiled happily at her, but she did not return my smile. She looked worried.

"Ann," she said, "people in this country do not usually masturbate in front of other people. It is considered offensive."

"Forgive!" I exclaimed. "I mean not to offend. In my country, women do often the self-loving before other women, sometimes even men."

She smiled a little then. "Your sexual customs," she said, "are quite radically different from any that my people generally admit. People do those things, of course. People do everything, one way or another. But the difference is that we all try to conceal it. Very few of us are as up front and frank about sexual matters as you are, Ann. That's one of the things about you that I find most strange and intriguing. You seem never to have had the kind of cultural conditioning that every one of our children absorbs almost as soon as it's weaned. With you it's as natural as an animal licking its privates. I find this endearing in a way, but I must ask you to remember not to touch your genitals in the presence of other people. It would not be understood."

"I am sorry," I said. "Your customs are difficult for me, seeming not natural, seeming against the way of the Mother. I will remember." I covered myself up again and returned my attention to the teevy box, which was showing a long, boring interlude of cars going very fast and men shooting at each other. How strange, I thought, that people could enjoy looking at *that* but not enjoy witnessing one of the Goddess's best blessings. How could they hope to understand the divine essence when they pretended to hate the bit of it that dwelt in their very own bodies?

Indeed this was an unhappy world. Its people dwelt in paradise but treated each other and themselves as though they were evildoers in Hades.

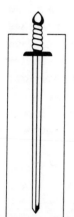

CHAPTER 5

SOON BEGAN THE PERIOD WHEN I BECAME SOMETHING like a schoolgirl, as these people would have said. I had to learn some basic skills that everyone in this world took for granted, as they took for granted their magic teevy pictures and their amazing cars and their clean hot water. I had to learn their letters.

Often the teevy box showed alphabet letters that I could not read. I begged Diana to teach me the holy skills of the letters, known only to the chief priestesses in my homeland. Diana showed me her alphabet and spoke the sounds for each letter. It was a simple system after all. I had only to put the symbols together with the sounds. I wondered if the priestesses at Themiskyra used the same alphabet.

Diana said I learned so fast that she was beginning to think me a genius. Soon I was trying to write some words of my mother tongue, spelling them in Diana's letters by their sounds. When Diana saw this, she asked me to prepare some pages of my own language written phonetically, with translations. This task occupied me for many hours and helped to pass the weary days of inactivity.

While my leg healed, I stayed inside Diana's house. I felt safe there. I was intimidated by the strangeness outside: the sterile streets, the noisy vehicles, the alien people passing by. Diana brought home amazing clothes for me. There were pants, shirts, special undergarments, even special sleeping garments called pajamas. Everything was colorful, soft, deliciously smooth, like no clothing I had ever worn. Diana gave me a beautiful shiny red comb for untangling my hair, fine snow-white sandals for my feet, and a belt with studs of gold and silver, like stars. This even induced me to lay aside my old sword belt, although it remained beside my bed. So many wonderful treasures came through Diana's generosity that I felt almost as deeply obligated to her as to my own mother. After all, I owed her my life too.

Diana also brought me the materials used by women of her country to deal with their moonblood, although Diana as a Crone kept her own moonblood within and had no further use for these things. There were curiously fashioned soft white pads and absorbent plugs to insert into one's inner temple. I learned that the women here do not sit in menstrual huts or give their blood back to Mother Earth to nourish Her universal life spirit. I wondered if that was why the land seemed so sterile. For women not to honor the moon or make rituals for their moon-time seemed highly irreligious to me. Diana's country was an unwomanly place indeed.

I saw no other people during this time except Diana's sister-son Jeff, the healer, who came now and then to change the dressing on my leg. Diana asked me not to talk too much to him. She told him that she was working on a "story" about me, but it was not yet ready. She promised him future revelations. I knew he was curious, for he asked me about my scars. I said I had been in some battles, but I did not explain. I still feared that some of our sworn enemies, the Greeks, might be lurking some-where in this land.

One day when Diana was away on assignment, Jeff came early to examine me. I padded to the door in my new coral-colored pajamas, saw him through the glass, and let him in. He asked, "Where's Aunt Di?"

"Out of town," I said, as she had instructed me. I opened my pajamas and dropped the pants to the floor. Naked from the waist down, I sat in the armchair and extended my leg on the footstool. He set his bag on the rug and took out fresh bandages.

That morning I had been feeling lonely, homesick, weary of physical inactivity, and sexually inflammable. Watching Jeff's careful hands as he worked, I began to perceive him as an acceptable lover. When the rebandaging was finished, I reached between his legs and stroked his genitals, as is the custom of women of my tribe when they want to invite a man. To my surprise, not only his penis but his whole body went stiff. He drew away from me as Diana had done. O Mother, I thought, have I committed another offense against their strange negative sexual customs?

"You're very attractive, Ann," he said thickly, "but you know I'm a happily married man and I don't play around."

"What does happy married have to do with playing?" I asked. I could see no logic in his remark. I continued to stroke him in the way that men like. He began to breathe harder. He took a backward step, but by then I had risen to my feet and unfastened his pants with a quick snap of that convenient and marvelous invention called a zipper. I had his penis in my hand, and I could tell that he would back away no more. Everyone knows how that piece of flesh belongs to woman even though it is wrongly attached to man—for was it not taken out of woman's body in the beginning, and is it not still under her control? For the moment, his penis was not his but mine.

To my surprise, once he had entered me, he did not proceed decently, as men were taught among my people. He was crude, clumsy, and much too fast. He committed the ultimate offense, allowing himself to climax while still within my body. I was outraged. This was an intimacy of life generation that no man had a right to claim without a specific invitation. I shoved him away and stood up, panting, red-faced, torn by both anger and unfulfilled passion.

"You dare!" I cried. "I invited you to love, not begin child!"

Groping for his pants, he turned toward me a face of puzzlement like a small boy ready to cry. "You mean you aren't . . . you haven't . . . you didn't take any precautions?"

"I don't understand your word," I hissed. "You goat, you rooster! Your mother never teach you proper man love?"

"Now I don't understand," he said. "I'm sorry if I offended you. I'm sorry about the whole thing—God, am I sorry." He pulled his pants up.

Still unsatisfied and annoyed, I turned and limped away to my bedroom. I slammed the door and finished my climax with my own fingers. He came and knocked on the door. "Ann, I have to go now," he said. "Please forgive me. I didn't mean this to happen. I hope I can forgive myself."

"Go, good-bye," I said. It was clear to me that Jeff was certainly not the lover I wanted. I waited until I heard the front door close. Then I went to the kitchen, made some tea, and sat down to my alphabetical tasks.

▼ ▼ ▼

In the evening, when Diana returned, the telephone rang. Diana always answered it; I was instructed to let the answering machine deal with it when she was not home. After the call, she said, "That was Jeff. He says you are all right now and won't need any more medical attention. He says you can replace that bandage with one of the large Band-Aids."

"Jeff came today," I said. "I forgot to tell. He made love. Very useless. I sent away."

"He did what?" She seemed both horrified and eager to know.

"Made love," I repeated. "Is that wrong term? Stayed inside, like to begin child. Very useless. No good lover."

"Jeff seduced you? Oh, heavens. Marcia must never, never know."

"Marcia?"

"His wife."

"She would care? Not like?"

"Yes, Marcia would care very much. She certainly would not like." I thought, How odd these people are. A man so unskilled at love, yet she wants that one and no other.

I said, "Jeff not seduce. I seduce him. Men not decide such. But he made to begin child. Bad thing."

"You mean he might have impregnated you? That is bad. I don't suppose you've ever heard of birth control."

"What is it?"

Diana then explained to me the anticonception devices and medicines used by the women of her country. She showed me her old diaphragm and her pills.

I said, "For lovers who cannot learn control, my sisters use sponge from the sea. But most men learn control."

"I wish I knew where you came from, Ann."

"I wish, too," I said. "Then I return there and be no trouble to you anymore."

She hugged me. "Ann, dear, you're no trouble. Why, you've given me a consuming interest, a riddle to unravel. But I'm sorry that you're homesick. I wish I could give you back to that motherclan you love so much. It sounds wonderful, even if it's only a fantasy of yours."

That was when she managed to talk me into parting with my sword. I tried to explain that a warrior's sword was a sacred trust, never to be abandoned, but she swore that it would be back in my hands within three days. She wanted to show it to a learned man who might be able to find my home by studying my sword. Reluctantly, I allowed her to take it. I stood clutching my amulet bag in apprehension as I watched Diana's car drive away the next morning, carrying my sword.

She was as good as her word. The sword was back in three days. It seemed unharmed, except for a tiny nick out of the haft, which I had not noticed before. Diana said the learned man was still pondering the problem and would provide an answer soon.

Despite Jeff's shortcomings as a lover (I believe I have made a pun here), he was competent enough as a doctor. He was right about my wound. It had healed faster and more cleanly than any wound I had ever seen. Soon I was walking with little pain and only a slight limp. I was talking well, too. Diana professed herself astounded at the speed with which I learned her language. I explained that the thought-sensitive state made it possible. Without such a mental trick, it would have been slow going indeed. Diana didn't understand the thought-sensitive state. It seemed that all her people had either lost the knack or had never had it in the first place.

One morning she said to me, "Let's go out today, Ann. You've been cooped up long enough. You keep asking me where the food comes from. Would you like to see?"

This was exciting, if a little frightening. I would go forth with Diana in her car to see crowds of other people and strange sights. I ran to fetch my sword. Diana gently took it from me, saying, "You won't need that."

"I will! If I had not been armed, those men would have killed me. Have you forgotten?"

"No, I haven't forgotten. But we're only going a couple of miles, into town. There are no hoodlums there. No one carries weapons. It's against the law."

"A warrior does not go forth unarmed," I insisted. "I go with my sword or I go not."

"Then we'll hide it," Diana said. From her office she brought a fat cardboard tube longer than my arm. "You'll carry a mailing

47

tube, not a sword. Will you at least hide it in this, instead of wearing it?"

I agreed. The sword was sealed in the mailing tube. It was an awkward burden, but it gave me confidence.

What can I say about that first sight of the cornucopia that is taken for granted by the people of this land? The market shelves were piled high with colorful fruits and vegetables, like precious jewels in their ripeness, an abundance that no village anywhere in my world could produce all at once in the same season. The animals were already killed, cleaned, cut up, and presented in small pieces that hardly looked like real flesh. Unmoved by these miracles, people were calmly strolling through this paradise of victuals, receiving rich assortments of food with no more effort than it took to pluck a can or a bag from a shelf.

"Who does the real work?" I asked Diana. "Where grow these crops? Where the raising, fattening, and killing of animals? Where the cow mothers giving so much milk? Where the hen mothers laying such eggs? Where are butter churns, cooking pots, baking ovens, pickling buckets?"

"We never see those," Diana said. "There are gigantic factories where hundreds of people work together every day. The soups, for instance, are made in huge vats as big as a room in my house. The farms are hundreds or even thousands of miles away. Everything is collected into big warehouses, loaded on trucks, and carried to every store in the country."

"There are more stores? This is not the one central market?"

"There are thousands of stores like this one, and thousands more that are even bigger, all over the country. But you don't really know how big the country is, do you, Ann?"

"How many days' ride? Horse, no car."

"You could ride a horse from one seashore of this country to the other in perhaps six months, perhaps more."

I couldn't believe it. One country so big! Indeed I was far from home.

I felt even more removed from my home after the "parking lot incident," as Diana later called it. We came from the store with our bags of food and began to load them into Diana's car. In the car next to us were three young children and a man, who sat waiting while a woman pushed her grocery cart up and began to unload it. One of the little girls fidgeted and squirmed. Suddenly the man slapped her sharply, telling her to be still. She began to wail. The man slapped her again, saying, "Shut up!" She gulped, closed her mouth, and whimpered thinly.

"Leave the kid alone, Ed," the woman said in a weary tone.

The man got out of the car and swaggered over to her. "You tellin' me what to do?" he demanded harshly.

"No, Ed, I just . . ."

"Where's my scotch?"

She handed him a bag. He pulled a bottle out of it, looked at it, and abruptly slapped the woman just as he had slapped the child. "You stupid bitch," he said. "That ain't scotch, it's bourbon. I told you scotch."

He raised his hand again. The woman cowered against the car, expecting another blow, which never fell. By that time I had my sword out of the mailing tube, had spun the man around with an ankle shove to put him off balance, and had pinned him against the car with the point of my sword at his throat. "Men not hit women and children," I said.

"Who the hell are you?" he demanded, glaring through bloodshot eyes. He was about to attack me. I shoved his shoulder back harder and gave his neck a little warning prick. Blood trickled down to his collar.

"Men not hit women and children," I repeated. "Wrong."

"Mind your own goddamn business!" he shouted. I pricked him again. Then Diana was at my side, saying, "Come on, Ann, you mustn't do this."

"Damn right she mustn't do this!" the man blustered. "Call

a cop, you! Get her back to the bin where she belongs! What's she doing with that illegal weapon?"

Ignoring everything, I said, "You swear by whatever spirit you worship, never to hit women or children again—else I kill you right here."

He stared into my eyes and realized that I meant it. By way of encouragement I let him feel my blade once more. His collar was now quite red. I saw him begin to tremble.

"OK, lady, OK. Don't get excited."

"Swear," I said, tensing my grip.

"OK, I swear. I'll never hit anybody, so help me God. Satisfied?"

I looked at his woman, who stood with her mouth open, holding on to a grocery bag. "You remember," I said. "If he does criminal acts, I will find him." She nodded without closing her mouth.

I backed off slowly.

When I released him, the man scrambled into his car and locked the door. The woman finished loading her groceries, watching me curiously. Then she got in beside the man and they drove away.

Diana said, "What you did is against the law, Ann."

"It is not against the law for men to hit women? It is against the law for a woman to defend another woman from a man who attacks her? What kind of laws here, Diana? All laws invented by men?"

"Well, yes. Nearly all our lawmakers are men. But the law does provide for women's protection against physical abuse. That woman could report the man to the police and take legal measures against him, especially if he did her or the children any serious injury. Nevertheless, strangers like you shouldn't intervene, unless someone's life seems to be threatened."

"No police here," I said. "Who is protecting? In my country, women protect each other. I am a warrior. I defend."

Diana's lips were twitching and her eyes were narrowing, which I had learned to recognize as symptoms of barely suppressed inner glee. Suddenly she erupted in laughter. She bent over, pounding her fist on the hood of her car. I couldn't help laughing with her.

"You're a warrior all right," she gasped, wiping her eyes. "Ann, you're something else, you are. Superwoman. The Capeless Crusadress. The Maskless Avenger. Help of the Helpless. Whoo! I'll never forget the look on that creep's face. It was worth the price of admission. But seriously, Ann, you can't go around publicly threatening people with your sword. I knew we should have left that thing at home. If you do anything like that again, you could go to jail."

"Like in the teevy box?"

"Yes, like that. You wouldn't enjoy being locked up."

"That man should go to jail. What he does is against Mother law. In my country, no man may strike woman or child. No mother would allow a cruel man to be near her children."

"That man was probably the children's father," Diana said. "In the bad old days not so long ago, fathers had absolute legal control of their children and over women, too. Fathers could beat or even kill their dependents, almost at will. Now the laws are better. That woman could divorce her husband and keep the children away from him if he is truly abusive."

"She cannot simply say he is unworthy to be a father, send him away, and take another man?"

"Not that easily. She would have to go through a legal process that can cost a lot of money. Some wives think they can't afford it, especially if all the money is earned and kept by the husband."

"Your country is terrible," I said. "Men rape, kill, hurt mothers and children."

"Not all men," Diana said. "Decent people don't behave like that lowlife. Unfortunately, not all people are decent."

"Every day your teevy box is showing men how to be cruel," I said. "It will make them not decent."

Diana gave a rueful grunt. "I'm afraid you may be too right about that. Funny that it seems perfectly plain even to you, after minimal exposure, yet media people themselves do nothing but make lame excuses and go on escalating the violence. Many of us are bothered by that."

"In my country, the only violence is war, when we must fight to save our motherland, whether we want to or not. When we have defeated our enemies, war will stop forever."

"I've heard that line before," Diana remarked. "But let's try to find out more about your country, what say, Ann? Before either of us gets much older, we should start some serious research. Let's begin this afternoon."

And so we did.

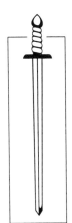

CHAPTER 6

WHEN DIANA SET OUT THE VOICE-RECORDING BOX, SHE asked me this time to speak in her language, English. I could manage the grammar fairly well by this time, but there were still many words lacking in my vocabulary and also many words for which I knew no English equivalents. For example, I did not know the English word for Greeks. At first I called them god-men, but that was not right because Diana thought I meant divine spirits. I had to explain that I meant only men who worshiped gods and neglected the Mother. Then I called them brute-men, to indicate that they were cruel. That was not right either, because she thought I meant men who were like animals. Finally we agreed that the Greeks could be described as father-dominant men. Diana told me that they seemed rather similar to the men of her own country.

Diana asked me all over again for the details of my former life. I described minutely how our clan system worked, how relatives related to each other, what we ate, what we wore, what our houses were made of. I talked about religion, agriculture, law, child education, marriage, warrior training, horsewomanship, the priestesses, the oracles—everything, down to our methods of building hearthfires, forming clay vessels, and joining skins to make garments. I described what little I knew of smithery, healing, winemaking, midwifery, and other special occupations. I recounted my entrance into the womb temple, the priestess's words, my rude awakening on the highway. Sometimes I cried. My heart remained sad at the loss of my mother and sisters and of my home. Diana comforted me and waited. The process stretched over many sessions. She wrote notes, and the folder containing them grew very thick.

One day she said, "I have a report on your sword. It is an extraordinarily valuable ancient artifact. The professor places it in Asia Minor with a tentative date around the third millennium B.C. Four or five thousand years, Ann! This sword is not archaeologically recorded. No one seems to understand its perfect preservation. The museum has offered $30,000 for it. Do you want to sell your sword for a big chunk of money?"

"No!"

"I thought not. But, Ann, we have to think about how you might make some money for yourself. In this world you need money to live. You will have to learn how. Evidently you will have to learn enough to find a job. If this former life of yours is a delusion, it's the most complete and consistent delusion I've ever heard. If it is not just a fantasy—well, the implications of *that* boggle my mind."

"I don't understand."

"If you're not inventing all this, the only other conclusion is that you've come from a time long ago and somehow materialized yourself thousands of years in the future—your future, that is. If so, your home no longer exists. But as far as we know, such a thing can't be. The only piece of hard evidence we have is your sword. I can't imagine how you might have come by that, unless you are the world's cleverest liar."

"A warrior never lies," I said firmly.

"I believe you, Ann. At least, I believe that you are telling the truth as you perceive it. The only problem is that what you perceive seems to be impossible. If it should be possible, then this is the first time in the history of the world that such a thing has happened. That makes you the biggest news story of this or any other century."

"You want to write about me?"

"I will, with your permission, Ann. But I have to gather all the data I can. That's necessary when one is talking about the impossible. May I take your amulets and have them analyzed too?"

I clutched my amulet bag in agitation. "These were placed on me by the Mother," I said. "I can't break Mother law."

"All right. Suppose I bring someone here to look at them. Would you allow him to handle them?"

"No him. If I let man touch my amulets, I am cursed. Only woman can touch."

"Then I'll find a female mineralogist," she assured me.

Several days later, Diana brought another elder woman to the house. I was naked in the living room, doing my exercises, but I wore a belt and one of the blood pads that Diana had given me. To my relief, the moonblood had come on me, showing that Jeff's sexual rudeness had no serious consequences. If I could have exercised outdoors as warrior women usually did, I would have worn nothing. I wore the pad out of thoughtfulness, to keep bloodstains off Diana's rug.

Diana's guest halted a few feet inside the door and stared at me. Diana, behind her, had a slight smile twitching at her lips as she introduced me to Dr. Ellen Fitzgerald, who had a great knowledge of stones. I greeted Dr. Ellen politely, bowing in deference to her gray hairs. Diana put a towel around my shoulders while the guest laid out a soft cloth on the table and asked me to pour out my amulet stones on the cloth. I did so. Dr. Ellen gazed for a few minutes, then put a little tube up to her eye and looked at each stone closely.

"Simple enough," she said to Diana. "An ordinary quartz crystal, a piece of carnelian, a chunk of magnetite, and a crudely polished tigereye. Nothing unusual about any of them."

"There's no way to ascertain the dates of their collection?" Diana asked.

"None. These minerals occur all over the world. They could come from anywhere, they could be any age. Most minerals are older than the human race in any case, you know. If they had settings, then we'd have something to go on. Metal workmanship can reveal a lot. But these are just pieces of natural stone."

"They are the Maiden, the Mother, the Crone, and the eye of the moon," I said. "These stones were put in the earth for the priestesses to use."

Dr. Ellen looked at me sidelong. "Whatever you say."

I said to Diana, "She thinks I am out of my mind."

Diana said, "I have not yet explained things to her. Later we shall see."

I picked up my black Crone stone and said to Dr. Ellen, "This stone is a personal limb of the Goddess. It will cling to the side of the Black Stone in the Mother temple of Themiskyra."

She asked me to repeat *Themiskyra*. Then she said, "I know that name, though you pronounce it oddly. I remember an old legend about a black stone in a shrine called Themiskyra. Pre-Greek, wasn't it? The stone was supposed to be sacred to the Amazon tribes around the Black Sea."

Suddenly Diana had her notebook in her hand. Clearly she was excited as she asked Dr. Ellen for more details.

"I heard several stories a long time ago," Dr. Ellen said. "I can't remember much. The Amazons were said to have worshiped a deity in the form of an aniconic black stone, possibly a chunk of meteorite. This may have been the same black stone carried to Rome in the third century B.C. as an image of the

Phrygian Goddess Cybele. Some claimed that after the religion of Cybele was suppressed by Christianity, six centuries later, the same black stone was taken to Mecca and served as the original Black Stone of the Kaaba. Early priests of the Kaaba were known as Sons of the Old Woman, and 'Old Woman' was one of the titles of Cybele and also of the Amazonian Goddess."

"Yes!" I cried. "Black Stone is the Old Woman Goddess who came from the stars. I have seen Her with my own eyes. This very eye stone has looked upon Her also." I picked up the one she called tigereye and pressed it to my breast. "She dwells at Themiskyra, the most holy place of my motherland. Oh, Dr. Ellen, do you know of my motherland, my people?"

"I only know a few ancient legends," Dr. Ellen said gently. "You know legends can be very misleading. They change as they are retold again and again for centuries. What makes you think your people live around the Black Sea?"

Before I could reply, Diana asked for reference works, articles, books, background information. She wrote down all of Dr. Ellen's suggestions. I could see that she was in hot pursuit of an idea.

Dr. Ellen promised to look up some other references and send Diana a new reading list. Between them, these two wise women seemed to be mapping out a path into my lost life. Overjoyed, I fell on my knees before Dr. Ellen, seized her hand and pressed it to my forehead. "Goddess grant that you will find a way to my home," I said.

Once again, as so many times before, I perceived that my natural gesture was overly emotional for the taste of this culture. Dr. Ellen withdrew her hand with a slightly embarrassed expression and awkwardly patted my shoulder. "I'll do what I can," she said. "Don't be too hopeful." Soon afterward, she took her leave.

My next profound experience came when Diana took me to the neighborhood library. I had thought Diana's book collection a marvel, believing that so many volumes of lore must have come from generations of patient accumulation. I imagined that Diana's private ownership of such a collection must imply great wealth. Then I saw the library. Whole rooms filled with books on every wall! Just counting the books would take a very long time. To read them all would take lifetimes. I stood amazed, turning slowly around to see it all.

"Diana, is this the central *byblos*—I mean, your country's temple of learning? Is all your people's magic knowledge here in this place?"

Diana laughed. "No, it's only the county library," she said. "A local facility, you understand? There are thousands and thousands of libraries like this one. The main library of the country is far away, in Washington, the government city. Every other large city has a central library, too. A big one. This one is very small."

A few people were walking calmly through this temple of learning. Some sat at tables reading silently. Diana consulted Dr. Ellen's list and began to choose books, leaving me to look around.

I dared not touch the precious volumes on the shelves, so I sat down at a table to wait. I watched a half-grown youth across the table. He was moving restlessly, munching the end of a pencil, shoving papers about in a listless, irritable way. He sighed often and pulled at his long unwashed hair. He gazed into space. He caught my eye and gave me a conspiratorial grin. "Dumb old history reports," he said. "Boring."

"What is history reports?" I asked.

"You kiddin'?"

"Please give me definition."

"Jeez. You sound like my teacher. You a teacher?"

"I wish to learn about what you are learning."

"I don't need this," the boy said. He picked up his books and papers and moved away to the next table, scowling at me. He slammed the books down roughly. I flinched. I felt that this careless youth had profaned a holy thing.

I got up and stood over him. "Rude boy," I said, "remember that you are privileged to know reading. Remember that you are blessed to be given teaching. Respect your books that you may respect yourself."

I walked away, leaving him with his mouth ajar.

I had learned another amazing lesson. Just as the people here starved their bodies for simple touching in the midst of an incredible feast of physical comforts, so also they often starved their minds in the midst of a feast of knowledge such as my world could not even have imagined. The library, which this idle youth took for granted and even disliked, was a fountain of information. The books could even be borrowed and taken away to be read at leisure. Diana already had an armful of them. Yet these treasure houses of knowledge were regularly used by only a relatively small proportion of the population. Freely available miracles of learning were disdained by many, who deliberately chose to remain even more ignorant than the poorest goatherd among my people.

A few days afterward, Diana took me to another temple of learning, a university. It was a beautiful place covering much ground, with grass and many tall trees and buildings that were like cliffs of stone. Diana said that we were to meet with wise men who knew diverse languages. I was to acquaint them with my mother tongue and also with what Diana persisted in calling my "gift" of thought sensitivity, though I tried to explain that it was not a gift but a skill, difficult to acquire and maintain.

We met with several learned men who lived in tiny cubicles cluttered with books and papers. One of them incessantly made smoke with the little sucking tubes called cigarettes. His cubicle was so hazy and evil-smelling that I could hardly bear to remain in it, even though I was getting used to the generally bad air of this world.

I spoke my mother tongue for each of the learned men. Each declared that he had no familiarity with it. Then came the difficult part. Each man spoke to me in several different languages. I was to hold my thought-sensitive state long enough to hear and translate the words into English. Diana and the men (professors, she called them) recorded my speech and wrote notes. The process went on for many hours.

At the end of the day, I was exhausted. On the way back to Diana's home, I asked, "Did I do well?"

She squeezed my hand and smiled. "Ann, you were wonderful. You gave them stuff they can write papers about for ten years. I hope they do write papers about it. Every little bit will help us."

Our next visit was to a police station, where a man made my fingertips dirty and pressed them on pieces of paper. I did not like the men there. Each one had a shooter gun, like the one that wounded my leg. They wore their guns on their belts, as if they were swords. I felt uneasy among these men without my sword. Diana had persuaded me to leave it in her car, because her country's laws said the police must take it away from me. Only these men were allowed to carry weapons. Bad laws those were, to deprive a woman warrior of her defense. In this land, only men were allowed to be warriors, and women could be intimidated by their implied threats of violence. Yet women were supposed to trust these armed policemen, just as women were supposed to trust the male healers and male priests who in their arrogance had erased the divine image of the Mother from women's minds.

On another occasion, Diana took me shopping in a place called a mall.

Here I discovered the true religious shrine of her people. In the bewildering crowds, I saw on almost every face the remote, satisfied expression that denoted an inner experience of worship. What they worshiped was the implicit vision of limitless acquisition.

The mall offered an overwhelming sensory experience where almost everything seen or felt was for sale. At first I was staggered by this environment. Unlike the holy caves at Themiskyra, which were artificially embellished but still mostly natural, the mall was completely artificial, a palace of wonders created by human beings. There were imitation ponds and fountains, thousands of brilliant colored lights, and a profusion of jewels, artifacts, garments, shoes, and other goods that reminded me of the abundance of foods in the supermarket. There were great treasure troves of objects more beautiful than the very flowers of spring: shiny, bright-hued things having no discernible purpose except to delight the eye.

Like a child, I was attracted to everything at once. I could not look enough to see it all. Soon I became almost paralyzed by so much feasting of the eyes. Diana, in contrast, ignored most of it while she led me firmly by the hand to a particular store.

Here, in a space a dozen times larger than Diana's large living room, thousands of bolts of cloth were for sale. They were dyed in colors unimaginable even to the Rainbow Goddess Herself, with patterns more intricate and complex than a magic labyrinth. When I followed their lines with my eye, I became caught in their webs and stood motionless until Diana pulled me away.

"Now, Ann, I want you to choose some fabric that looks like the clothes you used to wear at home. I want you to have some clothes that look authentic. Choose carefully."

"But my people never wore such fabrics as these," I said. "Where is the loomed flax, the ordinary sheep's wool, the softened leather? There is nothing here that my motherclan would recognize."

"I know it isn't the same stuff. We just want a rough resemblance. Think about it. Take your time."

Finally I picked out some coarsely woven grayish wool and some nubby yellowish-white curtain material that somewhat resembled homespun linen. Then I chose a bolt of brown suede material that looked and felt like the ideal we used to wish for when creating our garments of leather. It was as soft and pliable as a puppy's hide, a pleasure and a delight to the skin it touched. My clansister Niobe, who did most of our leather work, would have walked through fire to be able to achieve such a wonder.

More wonders were to follow. When we returned to Diana's house, she opened a closet and took out a little machine that could sew with marvelous speed. Instead of the hours of labor with rough needles and hand-twisted thread that was knotty and kinky, Diana could join pieces of cloth together in minutes with a nearly invisible seam. Now I could see how our beautiful garments were made before they were offered for sale in the stores. Diana could make her own garments whenever she wanted.

She cut out garment pieces according to my descriptions and sewed them together. Soon I had a small wardrobe of clothes that looked almost like my own home garb, though the materials were finer and the stitching far more elegant. One that was not very authentic was what Diana called my exercise outfit. She used the brown suede to make small coverings for my breasts, held on by thongs, and a crotch covering held on by my sword belt. Diana asked me to wear this instead of exercising naked, because she wanted to take moving pictures of my exercise routines—pictures that people could watch on the teevy box. She said her people could not watch if I was naked. So strange were the attitudes of her people.

One day Diana brought home a man who carried a large machine on his shoulder. Diana said this machine was a teevy camera that could take pictures of my exercises. We went outdoors, and the man filmed my morning routine. Later, Diana put a film into her own teevy box and showed me to myself.

Such magic worried me. I tried to explain my anxiety to Diana. "If my image is in the box there, strangers can see me and work bad spells against my image. It is just like"—I struggled for an analogy that she would recognize—"an image of your face in water. If someone stirs the water while you look at yourself, your image is broken, and this is like breaking the soul. Bad. Dangerous. My people never touch someone else's image. But if my image is in the box, evil men can see me and curse me. I will feel the curse through my soul image and perhaps get sick and die."

"Oh, no, Ann. That can't happen; it's only an old superstition. Look at all the people who appear on TV. They aren't afraid of curses or spells. Television doesn't work that way. You can turn off the picture and blank the people right out, but they don't die."

I had to admit that the women and men in the box seemed wholly indifferent to showing themselves to strangers. I trusted Diana, yet I couldn't help feeling a little uneasy about my exercise film. Throughout my life, I had been taught that personal images were vulnerable. In the end, it turned out that those teachings had been correct after all, though the eventual outcome of my appearances on television screens could not have been predicted by anyone—not by Diana, or myself, or the wisest priestess of my mother country.

Everything that happened to me in this new country was strange. But the strangest events of all began after the publication of Diana's book.

CHAPTER 7

I LIVED IN DIANA'S HOUSE FOR MORE THAN A YEAR while her book was in progress. Every day when she was home, we talked, I learned, she wrote. She arranged for me to do what she called my mind-reading trick for more language experts, each of whom signed a paper describing my skill. I tried to explain that it was not a reading of the mind but a reading of the tongue, because I couldn't understand the thoughts of others unless they were spoken. Later I began to suspect that my ability was beginning to decline as I spent more time practicing the eye-reading of thoughts in books.

Still, I correctly interpreted many obscure, ancient, or foreign languages spoken to me by all sorts of people, some of them racial types that I had never seen in my own land: yellow-skinned people with dark almond-shaped eyes; copper-skinned people with lank black hair; people from a faraway place called Africa, with skin almost as black as my Crone stone. Sometimes I would see such people in public, walking casually among those of the more usual range of colors, who never seemed to view them as anything remarkable.

I lost my fear of the barren streets. I went out every day, running for exercise, as our maidens and youths used to run over the hills above my village. I longed for a horse to ride. Diana said horses were not allowed in her neighborhood. Instead, she bought me a bicycle and taught me to ride it. That was beautiful! On this splendid little silver spiderweb of a machine I could fly along almost as fast as my lost Windeater could gallop.

I learned to ride the bicycle to the store and bring back groceries in its basket. I learned to count money and exchange it for goods. I learned to dress, to cook, to read signs, to ask directions, all as Diana's people did.

Even though I copied these alien customs and even though I loved Diana as a second mother, yet I remained homesick in my heart. Often I wondered what my sisters were doing and whether there had been any further Greek invasion of our land.

I first met some other members of Diana's family when her elder sister Dora invited us to dinner at her house in another town about forty miles away. Dora and her husband Elwood were Jeff's parents. Diana cautioned me not to tell them that I knew Jeff, either as a doctor or "in any other way," as she put it. She also enjoined me not to mention my own home or my former life. "I love Dora dearly," she said, "but the poor woman is the soul of conventionality. Anything unusual only upsets her, and you're unusual. She wouldn't understand you at all. As for Elwood"—she laughed to herself—"well, I guess you'll terrify him without half trying."

I promised to be circumspect, both for Diana's sake and because I still felt awkward about social customs. I never knew when I might do or say something that would seem gauche or intolerably rude. When in the presence of people other than Diana, I generally just watched and listened.

Unfortunately, when introduced to Dora and Elwood I made a mistake right away. I expressed surprise that Diana's own blood sister had a different clan name. I knew Diana's second name was Foster, but Dora's second name was Case.

"That's Elwood's name, of course," Diana explained in a low tone. "Married women usually drop their own fathers' surnames and take their husbands'. I returned to my father's surname—Dora's and mine—when I divorced."

"But where is the motherclan name?" I cried, bewildered.

"There isn't any," Diana said.

Dora and Elwood gave each other puzzled looks during this exchange, which left me as puzzled as they. I couldn't comprehend a people whose nomenclature completely failed to recognize the all-important blood bond of maternal descent. By the time I recovered from this surprise, Dora was already bustling in and out of her kitchen with drinks, dips, fruit, sliced vegetables, and squares of toast decorated with sausage and cheese. She was an earnest hostess.

Elwood was quite unlike the elder men I had known in my own country, whose lined and leathery faces showed their years of strenuous outdoor living. Under a nearly bald pate, Elwood's round face with its heavy-lidded eyes seemed bland, shiny, and smug. He looked younger than Dora, though Diana had told me he was some years older. He gave me a plump hand to shake, and let it lie in my fingers like a sack of jelly.

A little shorter, fatter, and grayer than her younger sister, Dora still showed features that noticeably resembled Diana's. She had none of Diana's air of repose, however. She fussed continually with bowls, plates, napkins, ice tongs, and things on trays. Paying little attention to the conversation, she jumped up and hurried to the kitchen five or six different times to fetch more snacks.

By contrast, Elwood sat perfectly still and allowed his wife to serve him the way a new mother serves her infant. He would hand her his glass, saying, "Another ice cube, dear," and she would provide it, even though the ice bucket was within his reach. She would move dishes closer to him so he wouldn't have to lean over. She offered him a cushion for his back, another toast square, a different kind of wine. If he chose to interrupt her speaking, which he did often, she immediately fell silent.

I thought it odd indeed to see a woman pampering a healthy, mature man as if he were as helpless as a tiny child or an exceptionally fragile invalid.

Elwood addressed most of his remarks to Diana, whom he seemed to find stimulating. To Dora he only gave mild-toned orders, like a benevolent king with an attentive lackey. When she talked, Dora kept telling us what Elwood thought about everything. She never said what *she* thought.

"I understand that you're one of those body-builder girls," Elwood said to me. "I must say you're prettier than I expected. I thought old Di must have taken up with some intimidatingly lumpy, pimply, lantern-jawed creature who knocks men aside like ninepins. Thank goodness I won't have to defend myself, ha-ha. You don't look like such a creature at all. Does she, Dora?"

"No, dear," said Dora, rapidly inserting toothpicks into cheese cubes.

"I have no reason to knock anyone aside," I said.

"As a rule I don't care for muscular women," Elwood went on, as if I hadn't spoken. "It seems unfeminine, you know. But some of the gals in those health-studio commercials on TV are quite attractive. Aren't they, Dora?"

"Yes, dear," said Dora.

"Elwood, you're pontificating again," Diana said with a disarming smile. "How about showing Ann your roses while Dora and I set dinner out?"

I could see that this struck the right chord in Elwood. Clearly, he fancied himself a master among growers of roses. I was taken out to his garden and given a half-hour tour of the bushes, with instructive commentary that I was not allowed to interrupt with questions. The flowers were nicely in bloom and really quite beautiful.

During dinner I perceived that relations between Diana and Elwood involved a great deal of teasing, most of which was good-natured but with an edgy undercurrent. Diana didn't like him; she tolerated him for her sister's sake. Elwood liked Diana, although she scared him a little. I gathered that he enjoyed her company more than that of his dutifully hovering wife, but he disapproved of her divorced status.

"Diana's entirely too independent for her own good," he said to me. "She's the family rebel, the black sheep, as it were. Every day she sounds a little more like one of those crazy man-hating feminists."

"Feminists aren't crazy, and they don't hate men," Diana said. "They just want the same respect, dignity, appreciation, and material rewards that society provides for men."

Elwood snickered. "Give up, Di. That's impossible. It's against the natural order."

I spoke up then. "The natural order is that women produce and nurture all human life and should be honored as our creators. Even animals recognize this law of the Great Mother."

Elwood gave me a hard look. "Oh-ho, what have we here? You're one of *those* women after all, hey? Forgive me, young lady, but when you're at my table you'll keep a civil tongue in your head, thank you. Dora, you know I don't like this kind of relish. Fetch the corn relish, please."

Dora immediately got up and went to the kitchen.

I said, "Isn't it her table, too?"

"No, it's not," Elwood snapped. "It was bought and paid for by me, like everything else in this house. Some of you women need to learn which side your bread is buttered on."

"Some of us prefer to butter our own bread," Diana said calmly. "Say, Elwood, did you see the article on famous rose gardens in last month's *Geographic*?"

He turned eagerly to his favorite subject, and I was left to reflect that I found both Elwood and Dora astonishing. Never could I have imagined such a relationship between mature adults. Both seemed incomplete, as if each needed the other to make a wholeness; yet even so, their sum did not amount to one well-rounded person.

On the way home I expressed this to Diana.

"I know what you mean," she said. "Probably I wouldn't bother with them if Dora weren't my sister. But they and Jeff are almost the only family I have left. Even without our consciousness of the mother-blood bond you talk about, family still means something. Dora is a good woman, with the kindest heart in the world. When we were children together, she looked after me like a mother. You wouldn't believe it now, but she used to be a tomboy with a lot of spirit. When she was in eighth grade and I was in second, one of the big boys took to bullying me. Dora met him in the playground and beat him up. Really. Sent him home crying, with a bloody nose. He never bothered me again. A few years later, her strength was lost, or buried, and she turned into what she was told was 'feminine.' Maybe she overdid it and went all the way to passive. But the least I can do for her is put up with her prig of a husband."

"Was your husband also a prig?" I asked.

"No. He was just plain selfish. Everything went well as long as I loved him enough to buy into his opinion that he was the center of the world. But when I began to need my own center, he couldn't allow me any space. So the marriage fell apart."

"What you call patriarchy seems to make men childish instead of truly powerful."

"You said a mouthful there, Ann. What they're afraid of now is that women might want to stop mothering them."

"But it's only natural for a mother to stop paying attention to men when she is occupied with her children. The offspring must come first. Even animals know that, including male animals. Why should grown men need such mothering? They should be more like the mothers, responsible for themselves, and for children, too."

"Some are, I guess. Maybe there's not enough of that kind to go around. I don't question Dora, though. She seems satisfied with what she's got."

"Perhaps he is an expert lover?" I suggested slyly.

Diana laughed and patted my knee. "Ann, dear, you're developing quite a wry sense of humor."

"Do all married men in this country behave like Elwood?"

"No, not all. But I suppose most would if they could get away with it. Elwood's not a bad person. His priggishness is partly Dora's fault. She has spoiled him with her overindulgence."

"Why?"

"I can't answer that, Ann. It's just part of the culture. Women often grow up believing that a 'good' wife has to indulge her husband's every whim. This is the ideal held up before both sexes. In practice it rarely works, of course. Still, women are given the notion that they should feel guilty if they fall short of the ideal. Dora has always been conscientious, so she's done her best to be one of those 'good' wives."

I had the impression that Diana had never thought the matter through in quite this way before. She was expressing ideas that were fairly new, even to her. My image of my motherland and its ways seemed to give her a different perspective on her own culture. Later on, this became very evident through her writing.

Following Dr. Ellen's suggestions, Diana researched the history of the Black Sea Amazons. There was not much information, even in those many library books, because the history was so old and forgotten. It was hard for me to believe that the Mother could have placed me in this strange, flawed world where men ruled so many centuries after my own time. It was hard for Diana to believe also, but her disbelief wavered as she listened to my descriptions. Everything I said matched or supplemented the information from books. Diana knew I could not have read those books earlier and made up stories from them. She trusted me not to lie.

I told her that the word *Amazon* sounded very much like "the people" in my native language.

"Some think it meant 'moon woman,'" Diana said. "Others think it meant 'breastless one,' because of an old story that each Amazon cut off her right breast in order to draw the bow straight."

"Nonsense," I said. "No clansister would cut off a breast. She would need it for her babies. Besides, breasts do not hamper the pull of a bowstring. Sometimes, though, our enemies would mutilate the corpses of fallen warrior women in that way, so they would go imperfect into the earth womb and be born again imperfect. It was an act of vengeance. 'Moon woman' is a name very close to 'the people,' since everyone knows that people are created by the moonblood given to us by the Mother. We see her sweet face in the moon every month as our blood tides rise."

The long, serene time of learning and working helped me to become accustomed to Diana's world, but all this changed after her book was published.

The book, *Amazon*, was an overnight success. Suddenly, Diana said, she found herself a celebrity instead of an obscure journalist. There was a storm of controversy, criticism, and publicity.

Some claimed that Diana told lies about me or that I told lies to her; either I was her dupe or she was mine. Some said the whole book was a feminist fantasy or an elaborate joke. Diana and I were called scheming lesbians, crazy ladies, space cadets. Some critics invoked the memory of a reincarnation hoax some decades earlier, the Bridey Murphy case.

Others took the book seriously, while granting that its unstated but implied premise of time travel seemed impossible. Many different theories were put forward concerning the situation in which I found myself. Prominent psychiatrists offered to assess my sanity. We received many requests for public demonstrations of my tongue reading, which people persisted in calling mind reading. Whatever their opinion of Diana's book may have been, people bought many copies of it.

This brought correspondingly large sales of my videotape, *The Amazon Workout*, in which I wore the pseudo-native costume Diana had made for me and wielded my sword. An amazing number of people offered staggering amounts of money for my sword, more money than I could picture or count. Fashion designers began to make and sell "Amazon kilts" costing more than forty times what Diana had spent for those few scraps of material. "Amazon amulets" in small leather bags were sold to women everywhere for $60 each. Mineral dealers tripled and quadrupled their prices for quartz, carnelian, magnetite, and tigereye, and still could hardly keep them in stock.

My real initiation into the bizarre condition of notoriety in this world came with our invitation to appear on television with a prominent talk-show host called Billy Bobb. The network, Diana told me, sent us first-class airfare tickets and a special dispensation from the airline for transportation of my sword. We were to be housed in a big-city hotel. We would be wined, dined, interviewed, and lionized. It sounded like a great adventure.

I had never seen a big city except on television. I had never been close to an airplane, even though the first things I had seen in this world were the eyelike lights of one, and I saw planes occasionally crossing the sky like high-gliding birds, and of course I saw them on television. But to fly in one, to be raised above the earth as on eagle wings—that was so exciting! I wearied poor Diana by asking her a dozen times a day how it would be.

When the appointed day arrived, Diana drove us a long way to an airport. There they were before my eyes: real airplanes! I was astonished to see how big they were. Huge metal houses, with gigantic wings stretching out a field-length on each side. I could not believe that things so enormous could raise themselves into thin air.

As we sat in the airport, I watched them take off and land. They did raise themselves into the air, and they did return safely to the earth, although it looked impossible all the while. Diana had explained to me how their fast forward motion provided lift over the airfoil shapes of the wings and how an aircraft could be controlled and steered, but still it seemed fantastic.

We were stopped by a guard when the package containing my sword went through the picture machine. "Is that a weapon?" he asked. Diana said firmly, "That is not a weapon. It is a very valuable ancient artifact, a museum piece." She flashed the special pass before his eyes, and the guard said no more. We proceeded, sword and all, to the waiting airplane.

Diana offered me a seat next to a window, from which I watched what is perhaps the most amazing spectacle that human eyes can see, because human eyes were never intended to see it: the solid earth falling away as one rises into the air like a bird. How often my clansisters and all our foremothers since the birth of the world had watched birds and longed to emulate their graceful soaring! Some of the priestesses said our honored dead were reborn as birds, which is why the flights of birds could provide us with auguries. Everyone hoped for an afterlife in bird form. And here I was, experiencing something like it, still in my human body, sitting at ease in a comfortable chair, rising into the sky in a flying house.

The airplane rose higher than any bird, far above the very clouds of heaven. I looked down on drifting islands, mountains, snowfields, and towering cliffs of cloud, looking as solid as glaciers. In the misty blue depths between and below them I could see the earth itself, forests of trees reduced by distance to a mere carpet of moss. Here I was in the remote, shining realm of the Sky Goddess Herself, a realm that had seemed forever forbidden to mere humans, a realm not attained by even the highest mountains. Yet as I looked around at my fellow passengers, I saw them taking this miracle very calmly. Few even looked out the windows. Diana herself was quietly reading.

A stewardess came to offer us food and drink. She would have been very pretty if she had not painted her face such unnatural, garish colors. (I never did get used to the appearance of women's makeup.) She looked at me and paused.

"Aren't you Ann Tyapay, the Amazon?" she cried. "And you must be Diana Foster," she added, turning to Diana. "I recognize you from the picture on your book. I've read the book, and I have the exercise tape. It's a great pleasure to meet you both. You've done a wonderful thing for women everywhere." She shook hands warmly with me, then with Diana. "You are very special people to me. My name is Charlene. If there's anything you want, anything I can do for you, anything at all, please let me know."

She went away and told other stewardesses, each of whom later came to shake our hands and praise our publications. Three of them requested our autographs, and it made me proud to be able to write my name in the letters Diana had taught me. For the first time I began to see the truth in Diana's view that just providing a detailed description of a nonpatriarchal culture would give many women in this country a new philosophy of human behavior to consider—one that they had never dreamed of before because they had no models. And now they were grateful.

When we began to descend over the city, I was astonished again. I could not believe that buildings made by humans could rise so far into the sky. At first I took them for unusual natural formations, but their squareness and sharp corners did not look natural. Then I realized that they had windows. Human beings

74

lived inside these giddy towers, these Titans' columns, these shafts and spearheads. And there were so many! Even the great temple of Themiskyra would have been lost among them. The city was bigger than any congeries of human habitations that I or my wisest ancestresses could ever have imagined.

We rode through the city streets in a taxi. Looking up at the buildings from the ground, I found them even more overwhelming. How could such structures exist? I knew it would be impossible to pile up stone walls to such heights. What held them together? I asked Diana. She said they were held together by steel, a magical transformation of the magical iron that my people were just beginning to discover.

The hotel was a palace, more beautiful than the most splendid temple, with a great central room whose ceiling was ten stories above the floor. There were elevators made of glass, so you could watch your rising and descending. We were given a large room with carpets that felt like mattresses, and mattresses that felt like clouds or feathers. Each of the two beds was big enough for six people. Vases of fresh flowers stood on all the tables. The vast adjoining bathroom had a pink, square sunken tub with mirrors and a matching bidet. I had never seen a bidet. Diana explained how it was used. I thought this such a practical idea that I wondered why bidets were not installed in all bathrooms.

There were also sliding glass doors opening onto a balcony overlooking a vista of the city. As night fell, I stood there entranced by the lights, a wilderness of stars below my feet. The city looked so beautiful that my heart wept with delight. I opened my suitcase and pulled out my running gear. As I was putting on my sneakers, Diana asked, "Are you going somewhere?"

"I am going out to run in this lovely city," I said. "Over there I see a dark area with trees. It looks like a good place to run."

"No, Ann. The city after dark is not a good place to run. You don't know which streets are safe. Bands of predatory men sometimes roam around at night, and if they find a solitary woman they may rape or even kill her."

Startled, I said, "But you know I can fight."

"Yes, but you can't fight bullets or half a dozen men at once. Remember what happened just before I found you. Men in this city carry guns like that one. You don't want to be shot again, perhaps fatally."

The gorgeous city lights looked a little dimmer. So in all this splendor lurked evil men who hated women! "And women all put up with that and agree to stay indoors after dark, so the men can have the streets to themselves?"

"Most do," said Diana, "except for those who go out in groups. Women who walk the streets alone after dark are usually taken for prostitutes."

"What are they?"

"They are women who lead very dangerous lives." She told me about these women who allowed men to masturbate into their bodies, asking for no sexual satisfaction for themselves but only for money. Sometimes they even allowed men to hurt them for payment. Most of their money, however, was turned over to other men, called pimps, who threatened or beat them if they did not obey.

Coming from a culture where such sex slavery was not even imaginable, I was deeply moved by the sufferings of these women. "But," I asked, "are the men of the city such bad lovers that they must pay women to accept them? Don't they know how to make women want them?"

Diana laughed. "Many don't," she said. "Some may find it too much bother. Some have odd sexual tastes that they feel embarrassed about. In any event, prostitution is called the oldest profession because it has been around for such a very long time."

"Not from my time," I said. "Why don't the prostitutes get organized together and beat the pimps who abuse them?"

"They just don't have the same ideas about women protecting each other. They think it would destroy their livelihood. They are afraid."

How terrible it was for the women of this world when they lost the Mother!

Diana ascertained that the hotel had an indoor running track, along with an exercise room, steam room, swimming pool, and other such amenities. I went there for my evening workout. Afterward we had a lavish dinner and went to bed. I was exhausted from so many new, stimulating experiences, yet almost too keyed up to sleep. The unfamiliar noise of the city kept me awake for a long time. I waited for the sounds of traffic in the streets to stop, but they never did.

The next morning, as we were breakfasting on our balcony, the telephone rang. Our network contact person was in the lobby. Diana invited her to come up. She was a frizzy-haired young woman in a black leather suit, with ponderous earrings that brushed her shoulders and a red notebook in her hand.

"I'm Jackie, Billy Bobb's researcher," she said. "I'm here to prepare the briefing for Billy Bobb. Since the show is scheduled for this evening, a script will have to be ready for him by afternoon." She accepted a cup of coffee, settled into a chair with her pen and notebook poised, and said, "Now, Diana, tell me about your book."

Diana looked surprised. "If you're the researcher, I'd assume that you must have read it."

Jackie giggled. "Oh, no. Researchers don't *read* the books. We only get a capsule—you know, the gist? Billy Bobb doesn't want anything too complicated. So if you'll just give me the basic idea in, say, a couple of paragraphs...."

Diana began to look rather frosty. I knew that look. She was displeased. "I don't think you can condense any six-hundred-page book into a couple of paragraphs," she said. "Especially a book like this, which raises complicated issues. We—Ann and

I—are making contrasts between our own culture, yours and mine, and a radically different culture with which she is familiar. There are many points that seem unbelievable, so I have done my best to document these thoroughly."

Jackie took a stick of gum from her purse, unwrapped it, and put it in her mouth. Chewing vigorously, she turned to me and said, "I hear you have an exercise tape. How would you say your exercises are different from all the usual aerobics and stuff?"

"My exercises are part of the daily routine for women warriors among my people. They are like what you call martial arts."

"Yeah? You mean like t'ai chi? I have a friend who does t'ai chi." Without pausing for an answer, she went on, "So, Ann, who are your people?"

"Diana believes they might be—might have been—Black Sea Amazons."

"OK. Who's that?"

Diana said, "The Black Sea Amazons lived in Asia Minor about the second or third millennium B.C. There were similar tribes, with similar customs, in North Africa, Galatia, and other areas."

"What do you mean, B.C.? You mean Ann here comes from a real old primitive tribe?"

Diana sighed. "I wish you had read the book. We think she may have come directly from ancient times, though that premise is very hard to accept. She has a unique skill with linguistics, a bronze sword several thousand years old, and she tells of living in a matrilineal, matrilocal society."

"You know, you can't use words like that on the program unless they're explained," Jackie said. "The audience wouldn't know what you're talking about. Remember, we're dealing with a mass audience. Billy Bobb might not know the words either, and he'd think you were trying to make him look dumb."

"Far be it from me to make Billy Bobb look dumb," Diana said dryly.

"So, what you're saying is that Ann came from this ancient time, whenever, to teach women about exercising and keeping fit?"

"Hardly just that," Diana said. "Ann tells with remarkable coherence of a society that worships a Great Goddess with only a minor assortment of subordinate male gods; where temples are controlled by priestesses, family ties are based on the maternal line, all property is inherited by women, and husbands move into their wives' homes. That's what matrilocal means. And because the Amazons were surrounded by hostile tribes who worshiped some form of God the Father and were always trying to invade Amazon territory, the girls were trained to be warriors and to fight along with the men, before they were allowed to be mothers."

"Oh. So these were people who don't believe in God."

"Yes, you might say so."

Jackie wrote busily in her notebook, while Diana rolled her eyes at me and gave a small, rueful smile. Then Jackie asked, "Ann, are you prepared to demonstrate some of your exercises for the camera?"

"Yes, if you like."

"OK, bring your exercise clothes. That might spark things up a little. Billy Bobb likes to have something more than talking heads. Let's see your antique sword."

I took it from its package and showed it to her. "Well, it's not really a thing of beauty, is it?" she said. "Did you find it yourself? I mean, like dig it up?"

"I did not dig it up," I said. "It was made for mc by one of our best smiths."

Jackie pursed her lips. "I'm kind of confused. You say this sword thousands of years old was made for you?"

"Yes."

"That would make you pretty old, wouldn't it? But you look only, maybe what, twenty-three?"

"I am twenty-five."

"Then how could you . . . " Jackie broke off and put down her pen. "Well, OK, ladies. Whatever you say. We'll hash out the rest later on. A car will come for you about three o'clock."

Diana took a copy of *Amazon* from her suitcase and handed it to Jackie. "I know there isn't much time," she said, "but you might understand our viewpoint better if you could read even a little."

Jackie took the book gingerly, as if she expected it to burn her fingers. "I'll see. But you know we have a pretty busy day, most days."

"I'm sure," Diana said, smiling. After Jackie left, she collapsed into her chair and began to laugh. "That's what's called research in the wonderful world of television, Ann. Oh, my. This adventure might be a great mistake. But we're into it now, aren't we?"

When we arrived at the studio, it was as busy as a nest of ants. No one seemed to know what we were doing there or where to put us. By chance we encountered Jackie, who recognized us. She went off to tell someone that someone else had ordered the services of the makeup department for us. She advised me to put on my exercise costume. When I had done so, a man in a smock came with a jar of flesh-colored paste to smear on the exposed parts of me.

"What's that?" I asked, backing away.

"Body makeup, honey," he said. "You don't want to go out there with your bare skin showing."

"Why not? It's my skin. There's nothing wrong with it."

"Just doesn't look good under the lights, dear. Besides, you've got those scars. You don't want the whole world to see them."

"They are honorable scars," I insisted, fending off his hand.

"Come on, I'm just doing my job," he said edgily. "If you go in front of the camera looking like a used coffee filter, it's my ass that gets chewed. So don't give me a hard time, OK?"

I shrugged and let him do his job. For all his irritable manner, he was deft and gentle at rubbing on the colored ointment. I was beginning to enjoy the process, when Billy Bobb himself came into the room with several other people. I recognized him because Diana had pointed him out to me on the television screen. He was a short, pudgy, sweaty, rapidly gesticulating individual whose hyperkinetic manner here contrasted sharply with the relaxed image he projected on the screen.

"So this is the fitness girl," he said. "Very nice. Now, honey, you're going to do a little exercise routine for us, right? If you need music, just give your tape to Ben here and he'll take care of you. The exercises are supposed to be self-defense, right? So maybe I'll pretend to attack you and you can self-defend, OK? All right. Now I understand that you come from some godless people who worship some kind of she-demon."

"Her Great Goddess is not a she-demon," Diana said. "She was the primary deity of ancient peoples in the prepatriarchal age. In the oldest myths, she was the creator of the world."

Billy Bobb jerked spasmodically, gave Diana a quick glance, and asked one of his aides, "How did she get in here?"

Jackie hastily flung herself forward. "Mr. Bobb, this is Diana Foster, the author of the book."

"What book?"

"You know, *Amazon*. The book you're going to be discussing."

"Oh, yeah, right. You got that script ready for me, honey?"

"Yes, sir, Mr. Bobb. Coming right up."

To Diana he said, "No offense, dear. Diana, is it? See you later, then." He turned and bustled out with his retinue.

Diana rolled her eyes to the ceiling, and we both began to laugh. I made a mental note: the more often strange men address you by love names, the less they love you.

Communication was not much improved during the briefing session, which coincided with a meal of sorts. Billy Bobb seemed increasingly inclined to view us as fraudulent people with an antibiblical (and therefore demonic) religion. But he sat next to me and continually touched me, rubbing his hand over my bare arm or leg, nudging me when he made a joke, kneading the back of my neck. His fingers crawled crudely and clammily. Finally he put his arm around me and reached under my garment to poke at my breast. Everyone else in the room was studiously looking elsewhere, except Diana, who was watching me with some amusement.

I plucked Billy Bobb's hand out of my clothes and pinched his little finger backward. He let out a sharp breath and began to squirm. I increased the pressure. Now he was pulling frantically to get his hand away from me. I gave it a last hard squeeze and let go. He stuck the injured hand in his pocket and did not use it again. He watched me sidelong, out of narrowed eyes.

Questions designed to lead into Diana's main themes were written down. I rehearsed a bit of my exercises, of which Billy Bobb said he wanted "three minutes, tops." He was annoyed when I said I did not work to music. "We'll give you a little background music anyway," he told me. "It always makes things go better. I mean, we don't want three minutes of silence, do we, sweetheart?"

During the live broadcast, Diana acquitted herself very well. It was clear that Billy Bobb was disposed to needle her or to mock her descriptions of a matriarchal society whenever he could. He was quick-witted about it, but she parried his frivolities with a serious, scholarly air that made her seem more credible than he. He began to sound more mean-spirited than amusing. He was intelligent enough to know this, and it bothered him.

When he turned to me, he was sweaty and somewhat flushed under his makeup. He said, "Now, Ann the Amazon, please tell our viewers what it's really like to live in a village where women do the fighting and nobody worships God."

I said, "First, women do not do all the fighting. Men are warriors, too. Men and women go together to battle. If only men fought, we would not have enough able-bodied warriors to defend our land. Second, our people do not know the God you speak of. We worship the Mother, who created all that lives. She is to be found in every womb of earth, sea, and heaven. Women themselves embody the Mother. Men do too, though less so, because they are woman-born. The Mother is the life force extending through all nature from generation to generation."

"Very eloquent," Billy Bobb said. "I'm sure there are a lot of feminists out there happy to hear that it was a woman who created them, not God. Of course, most of us take a more traditional view. But you haven't told me what it was really like to live there, way back in prehistoric times. Incidentally, your English is incredibly good, for a cave woman who just learned it less than two years ago."

"Thank you," I said, ignoring his irony. A new idea occurred to me, which had not been discussed earlier. "I'll tell you what it was like," I said. "When I came here to your city, I learned that women cannot walk alone in the streets by night or even by day in some places, because they have constant fear of men who may rape, rob, abduct, or kill them. And young children are never safe from men in this city. Both girls and boys must be guarded every minute, day and night. That is not civilized.

"My people did not have your beautiful lights, your tall buildings, your miraculous stores, your wonders of communication and engineering. But no woman, no child, was ever threatened with harm anywhere, at any time, in any part of my country. It would never occur to even one of our men to attack a woman or a child. It would never occur to any woman or child to fear a man. That is civilized."

Diana clapped her hands and cried, "Well said, Ann." Billy Bobb fidgeted a little and glared at her.

"I understand," he said, his smile quickly returning, "that you warrior women were well trained to defend yourselves against men if they did forget themselves and become dangerous and that you're going to show us some of the training exercises you used." He did not mention my videotape, which he was supposed to lift and display to the camera at this point. Nevertheless, I picked up my cue.

"Yes," I said, "but we were not trained to defend ourselves against our fellow countrymen. That would never have been necessary. No man attacked us except the God-worshiping strangers from the outlands."

With this I arose and walked to my place. A heavy, thumping rock music came from somewhere, fitting the tempo of my movements not at all, but I tried to ignore it. I went through approximately three minutes of the routine and was ready to stop and bow, as I had been instructed. Then came what was afterward known as "the incident."

Billy Bobb, wearing what was called his famous cute-mischievous expression, rose from his chair behind me and tiptoed into camera range, one finger on his lips, his eyebrows comically waggling. He meant to "attack" me, to show how I might respond to surprise aggression. Because of the raucous music, I could not hear him. Because of the blinding lights before my eyes, I could not see his shadow approaching. Moving quite fast for a man so fat and out of shape, he suddenly snapped one arm around my throat and simultaneously yanked one of my arms up my back to immobilize me. It didn't feel like a joke. He threw his ill-concealed hostility into it, and his grip was hard and painful.

Unfortunately, I reacted immediately according to my home training and not according to my recent indoctrination into patriarchal taboos. In a split second, my free hand whipped back into his crotch, clutched his genitals in an iron grip, and administered the twisting yank.

That was what we were all taught to do, without thinking, when seized from behind by a male enemy: go for the most vulnerable part of his body and hurt it as severely as possible. With a certain amount of pawing and horseplay and jokes, our brother warriors had let us practice on them, as long as we didn't really squeeze. They practiced it too, of course.

The effect on Billy Bobb was electric. He screamed and let go of me, whereupon I, still clutching him, whirled around and administered a hard kick to his kneecap as he was doubling over. That was the follow-up move; years of training had made it as natural to me as breathing. Under the camera's eye, Billy Bobb groveled on the floor, agonized, whimpering, tears starting from his eyes. I stood over him, wondering what would happen next.

I saw people rushing around wildly behind the glass separating us from the control booth. The camera operators gestured violently to me to move away from Billy Bobb's writhing body. I did so, walking back to my chair with as much dignity as I could muster. The camera followed me.

A different announcer was there, saying unctuously that Billy Bobb was a little inconvenienced at the moment and would be back soon. Meanwhile, a few commercial messages . . .

The commercial break went on for nearly ten minutes while they tried to get Billy Bobb on his feet. He screamed that he was lamed for life. He wanted me arrested immediately. "Assault and battery!" he yelled. "You all saw it!"

"The whole world saw it, Billy," a man from the control room said. "We didn't get it zapped. And it looked like you attacked her."

Billy Bobb stopped thrashing. "You didn't *what*? What are you saying, you fuckin' nincompoop? You mean to stand there and tell me that was *seen*, you asshole?"

The man nodded. Billy Bobb gave a final shriek and hobbled off the set, supported by three stagehands. He was howling threats, profanities, and inarticulate sounds of outrage. He had had it; he was out of this fuckin' business; never again would he come anywhere near the fuckin' freaks they wanted him to interview; he was going to sue everyone: me, Diana, her publisher, the network, the cameraman. Still declaiming at the top of his voice, he vanished into the distance, not to be seen again.

The other announcer quietly finished the interview in Billy Bobb's place. "Well, Ann," he said to me, "you certainly did show the world how an Amazon protects herself from attack from behind by a man. And of course, you were right; it is the most effective defense."

I was feeling abashed by the incident until I glanced at Diana, expecting to see disapproval in her face. Instead, she was smiling a small Mona Lisa smile, and she winked at me.

The next day, "the incident" was news. There were jocular headlines: "Amazin' Amazon Pulls Billy's Bobb"; "Billy Bobbles, Attacks Wrong Gal"; "'Castrating Woman' Almost for Real on the Billy Bobb Show."

Our telephone began ringing at seven in the morning and barely stopped all day. Diana handled most of the calls, which were from reporters. She explained that I had acted instinctively, without conscious intent, and that I deeply regretted the incident. (Actually, I didn't.) Many callers wanted to know if she was my press agent. Few realized that she was the author of *Amazon*. Strangest of all was the way the press had suddenly lost interest in Diana's book, preferring to talk at wearisome length about the relatively trivial issue of my encounter with a television star. Now I was the celebrity—and for such an absurd reason!

Billy Bobb was in the hospital, issuing no statements on the advice of counsel. It seemed that his kneecap was broken. Other injuries were not mentioned.

In the afternoon, Jackie called from the lobby. Diana said she could come up, but only if she were alone. She came, this time arrayed in a leopardskin print with ropes of blue beads. She walked directly to me and hugged me.

"All I want to say is thank you," she said. "You don't know how many times I've wanted to do the same thing to that fat bastard. I never could stand him. When he comes back to work, I'm quitting. You gave me the courage. Good luck to you. If he ever tries to hassle you legally, call me. I'll even lie on the witness stand for you if necessary. Now, you never heard me say any of that, but it's true anyway. Good-bye." She handed me her card, kissed my cheek, and left in a jangle of beads and a swirl of perfume. She still hadn't opened Diana's book and probably never would.

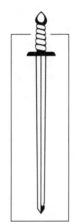

CHAPTER 8

"The incident" had a number of consequences, some serious and some silly. Any appearance on a major television program seemed to make one automatically a focus for the attention of many decidedly strange people in this strange land. Such people often took a proprietary interest in one's personal business, no doubt encouraged by the national habit of reporting on the private lives of those in the public eye.

Diana and I began to receive letters from people who pretended to know all about me because spirit guides had told them or because my whole life story had been "channeled" to them. Some said my people were not Black Sea Amazons but dwellers inside a mountain called Noella on the planet Venus. Some said I was a time-traveling Atlantean. Some said I was a vampire. Some said I was a serpent goddess from outer space, disguised in a human body that would self-destruct at the end of the year. Some claimed I was a she-demon from Sheol, a biblical hell, and my mission was to destroy all the men on earth after storing enough frozen sperm to keep the race of women going. Some declared that I was the Savioress or a female Antichrist come to announce the imminent end of the world. One told me that I could easily get back to my people by clicking my heels together three times and repeating, "There's no place like home," but I would have to be wearing the right kind of shoes.

We laughed over letters of this sort and then threw them away. Others we answered, one way or another. Many were business offers or requests for public appearances, usually involving "exposure" but no payment. Many were personal communications from women about the frustrations of their lives, their struggles to raise their children, keep their jobs, or escape from abusive men. They wanted us to tell them what to do. Other women wrote of their own convictions concerning the Goddess, whom they had discovered in their own souls or in private historical researches. Some wanted advice on establishing Mother temples with appropriate forms, decorations, and rituals.

In the latter category came a letter one day from Matilda Bloodworth, who, Diana told me, controlled a vast commercial empire and was one of the richest women in the country. She was semiretired now and lived in seclusion. Rumor had it that she was an invalid, but her illness was not publicly specified. She wrote:

Dear Mss. Foster and Tyapay:
I would like to meet with you to discuss the possible endowment of a religious institution based on your researches and experience. I do not travel much at present, but I will be more than happy to pay your expenses if you will be so kind as to visit my home on October 30 next, at high noon. I look forward to your reply.

> Most sincerely,
> Matilda Bloodworth

"I suppose this is in the nature of an imperial summons," Diana said. "I know nothing about this woman except what I read in the papers. But it can't do any harm to visit her. You might enjoy the trip and a brief glimpse into the life-style of the very rich."

"Yes, it sounds interesting," I said.

So we planned a journey to the Bloodworth estate at a time when the fall colors (as these people called them) were most intense. The brilliance of autumn trees in this part of the country was quite incandescent, much more colorful than the forests of my motherland. Even the profusion of spring flowers could not compete with these brighter colors: glowing gold, orange, lemon yellow, and blood red, mingled with the last greens of summer.

On the way I exclaimed over each new vista of brilliantly colored hillside, while Diana smiled at my delight. I must say there were many aesthetic compensations for the emotional unpleasantnesses of this world. Prominent among them was the joy of traveling along a highway on a sunny autumn day, the body quite relaxed but still moving at great speed, surrounded by the Mother's blazing banners of harvest time.

Sometimes, when there was almost no traffic, Diana allowed me to drive the car for a while. She had taught me to drive, but I could do so only illegally, for I was not officially a citizen and had no driver's license or other documentation. People here set great store by various papers proving that you existed. It was not enough just being physically obvious.

I thought this perverse, until I remembered the custom of my people of withholding a name from an infant no one wanted so that it would be considered nonexistent and would be allowed to die. On the rare occasions when a mother birthed a deformed, underdeveloped, sick, or otherwise defective baby, she could refuse to name it or to baptize it with her milk. Thus it would not be fed, would be viewed as a nonperson, and would soon perish. The names of things are so often thought important parts of their being. Many people here thought it essential that their names be written in stone on their graves, even after they had ceased to exist.

Matilda Bloodworth's estate was surrounded by an eight-foot stone wall that had a gate guarded by a man in uniform. He took our names and made a phone call, then he waved us on. We drove for a mile or two along a shaded lane and came to a lovely green rolling pasture behind a white fence. There stood a dozen of the creatures I loved most in the world after my own clanspeople—horses!

"Oh, stop, stop," I cried to Diana. I jumped from the car and ran to the fence. Curious, some of the horses left their grazing and drifted slowly toward me. First to arrive at the fence was a black mare who so closely resembled my long-dead Windeater that she brought tears to my eyes. There she was, alive again: the same delicately dished face, the same glowing dark eyes as big as plums, the same long mane, covering all her neck. I stretched out my hand, and the mare nosed it with the same caress of greeting that Windeater used to give me.

Diana came up and found me weeping, petting the black mare. "Look, it's my Windeater come back to life," I said. "This mare is exactly like her, exactly! She has the same mannerisms, stance, form, everything!"

Diana gently took my arm to draw me away. "Perhaps not exactly, Ann. You've been very lonely for your mare, I know. Any animal that resembled her would trigger these memories."

"No, no, it's more than resembling. I know her, I tell you. And look, she knows me, too." The mare was nuzzling the side of my head, just as Windeater used to do.

Diana looked unconvinced. "Well, she's a beautiful creature, at any rate. Come along now, or we'll be late for our appointment with Her Imperial Majesty."

Soon the house came into view. It was a great sprawling structure built in what Diana called the Tudor style, with many wings, terraces, chimneys, and small-paned windows. We were admitted by a butler wearing formal attire and white gloves. He suavely conducted us to a pair of double doors, opened them, and ushered us into a room so long that its far end looked dim. "Madáme has asked that you await her here in the museum," he said. "She will be with you shortly." So saying, he withdrew and closed the doors.

The room had glass cases along the walls and in the center of the floor. A large table near the windows bore a detailed scale model of a building. It was shaped like a pointed oval, with rounded, tunnel-like galleries running down each side, and an elaborate glass skylight covering the central space. At one end of the model stood a short, squat tower.

My attention was drawn to one case in particular, which contained objects seeming strangely familiar to me. Coming closer, I recognized a sword almost identical to mine, except that it was in terrible condition: nicked, corroded, tarnished, the handle half eaten away. It looked as though it might have been buried for a thousand years or more. Yet on studying it, I thought it might have been forged by the same smith who had made my weapon. Next to it hung a copper necklace and crown set with Crone stones, such as my people customarily buried on the corpse of a queen or high priestess. They were also eroded and green with age but recognizable. I knew that workmanship. Nearby lay a couple of blackened silver buckles such as my clansisters used to fasten their cloaks and a few small clay Goddess figurines such as my mother set up on her hearth to watch over the bread baking and butchering. Each Hearth Mother figure was always given a tiny dab of the flour or the blood.

My own blood ran cold at the sight of these things. "What kind of place is this?" I cried to Diana. "Artifacts that I have seen before, a mare identical to Windeater! Is this Bloodworth woman a great priestess? Does she know about my people? Has she a magic?"

"I think her only magic is unlimited money," Diana said. "She certainly has some remarkable things here. Look at this life-size Isis statue. How she got that out of Egypt I can't imagine. If it's genuine, it must have cost a fortune."

I was so shaken by the sight of familiar things in such an unfamiliar place that my legs felt weak. I sat down on a leather chair by the fireplace and knotted my quivering hands together.

I jumped up as the double doors opened to reveal Matilda Bloodworth in person. She was a regal-looking Crone with silver-white hair and a deeply wrinkled face set with keen, snapping blue eyes. She wore a long violet-blue gown and leaned on a silver-headed cane. She came slowly into the room, limping heavily, propping one hip against her cane.

"Welcome, ladies," she said. "I see you have already found something to interest you here in my little collection." She shook hands with each of us, then settled carefully into a chair facing us. "As you perceive, it is a collection of Goddess images and artifacts from matriarchal or presumed matriarchal cultures. I have been assembling these things for forty years."

"How can you have such things from my own people?" I burst out. "Even a sword like mine!"

"Yes, the sword," she smiled. "It's one of the few known surviving Scythian swords. I hope to compare it with yours, which I understand accompanies you everywhere."

"It is in our luggage," Diana said. "Ms. Bloodworth, is that the primary reason for your invitation?"

"Call me Mattie," she said. "No, it isn't my primary reason, though of course I'm very interested. I told you that I am considering endowing a religious center—a temple. You see the model there on the table. The plan is to make it the very first temple in these times dedicated exclusively to the Goddess. I need your advice on interior decoration, setting up the organization, and training the priestesses."

"I can't be much help with that," Diana said. "Ann would know more than I."

"But I have not been a priestess," I protested. "I know only a small portion of their lore."

"Yes," Mattie said, looking at me sharply, "but you have been there. Of that I have no doubt. Now that I see you, I am even more firmly convinced that you speak the truth."

She invited us to study the temple model, pointing out that it was designed in the shape of a yoni and would include underground crypts and catacombs furnished as earth-womb chambers, meditation rooms, and places of initiation. The long glass-roofed central courtyard was to be embellished with fountains, shrubs, and exotic flower and herb gardens, planted in female symbolic patterns. There would be consulting rooms for a staff of salaried adviser-priestesses who would help women with their personal problems—for free. There would be massage rooms, ritual rooms, classrooms, an extensive library, an art gallery, a theater, a museum. She hoped to append a small but complete obstetrical hospital.

"I have purchased the land and engaged the architect," she said. "I have not so many years left to me that I can afford delay. This project has become my obsession. My children say I am crazy. Of course they are angry because it will bleed off a large part of their inheritance. But Goddess knows they are rich enough already."

The butler announced lunch. With Mattie leaning on his arm, he conducted us to a cavernous dining hall with a very long table, three lonely-looking places set at one end of it. There was a bright fire on the hearth. Tall windows opened on a vista of hills clothed with red and gold trees. We were given a delicious lunch by silent, soft-footed servants in crisp lace-trimmed uniforms, while Mattie went on talking of her temple.

"I hope you will spend at least the next couple of days here," she said, "so we can talk at leisure. I have something special planned for tomorrow. It is All Hallows' Eve, which the Celts called Samhain—the Feast of the Dead, the Night of Souls, the Crack Between the Worlds, when 'witches' called up the ancestral spirits, whose dry bones spoke and gave oracles or who appeared in the form of owls or cats. Much as it was diabolized, it is one of the few remaining holidays surviving through all the Christian centuries from pagan and matriarchal times. I have a small group of like-minded women who meet here on such occasions to celebrate in the ancient manner. I'm sure you would enjoy it. I would be honored to have your company for the ceremony."

Diana said, "We will be glad to stay for that, but we really must leave on the next day. Work presses."

"I understand," said Mattie. "Meanwhile, you are free to roam the house and grounds. There is much to see. Ask the servants about anything that interests you. If you want a guide, I will provide one."

"I am very interested in your horses," I said eagerly. "One in particular, the black mare with the long mane. She could be the twin of the mare I used to ride—at home."

Mattie smiled. "Yes, your Windeater. I remember. Then we shall arrange for you to ride her here. She is a fine mare, purebred Arabian. Her name is Melanie. Since I am unable to ride anymore, the horses are just pets for me. They are ridden by my grooms and my guests. After lunch I will send one of the maids to your room to show you to the stables."

Presently we were conducted to a pair of adjoining bedrooms, where we found our clothes already unpacked, pressed, and hung up. Each room had an enormous canopied four-poster bed and other furnishings of a style that I had never seen before. Diana said they were priceless antiques.

I entrusted Diana with my sword so that she and Mattie could study it together. Then I dressed myself in a thick flannel jacket and tight jeans for riding. I was almost quivering with excitement. To feel a horse between my legs again would be thrill enough; to feel one so much like Windeater would be a bliss that I had never hoped for again. I had long since given up believing that my life in this world was only a dream, from which the Mother would soon wake me. It had gone on too long and had become too complex to seem dreamlike anymore.

A gentle knock at my door announced a young woman in dark blue slacks and shirt, with a blue and white patterned sweater. "Good afternoon, Ms. Tyapay, my name is Rose," she said. "I have come to guide you to the stables." She led me through the maze of corridors and stairways of which this house seemed to consist to a long, high-ceilinged hall ending at a side door.

Halfway along the hall, we passed the oddest door I had ever seen. It was flanked by two huge stone statues of the Goddess whom Diana called Isis, eight feet tall even in their seated positions. Each bore a stiff-looking infant on Her lap and negligently suckled it, with an expression of one lost in thought. The broad closed door between these two images was mat black, so intensely black as to resemble a hole instead of a solid panel. It had no doorknob or lock that I could see. In the center of this door floated a large five-pointed star, three feet wide, drawn by interlaced ribbons of a curious material sparkling with iridescent lights and reflections just beneath its silvery surface. My attention was caught by this design because I had seen it before—in the great temple at Themiskyra.

"Wait," I said to Rose. "Where does this door lead?"

She paused and smiled. "We are told never to open that door to visitors," she said. "Most of the servants don't even know how to open it. But for you, it will be opened tomorrow. It leads to Madáme's ritual room."

"Ah, the All Hallows ceremony."

"Yes. As it happens, I am one of the group privileged to take part. We are honored to have you among us, and I am very much looking forward to it."

We went on outside and followed a white gravel pathway to the paddocks and stable buildings behind the house. There Rose pressed a bell near the mounting block, smiled at me, and left. The bell summoned a groom, who led the black mare Melanie toward me. She now wore a light bridle and a strange little saddle with two iron hoops dangling down her sides, suspended by thin leather straps.

"What is this?" I asked, seizing one of the hoops.

Keeping his head bent, I thought perhaps to conceal his surprise at my ignorance, the man answered from under his broadbrimmed slouch hat, "A stirrup, ma'am."

"What is it for?"

"To put your foot in."

"Please take it off."

"If you say so, ma'am."

While he removed the stirrups from the saddle, I petted Melanie, combed her mane with my fingers, and talked to her. It was wonderful to touch and smell her—that well-remembered silky feel of horse coat, that sweet musky odor of horse skin. I was so preoccupied that I hardly noticed the groom's slow response to my assumption of the customary mounting position. As my people had always done when helping one another to mount, I stood at the mare's shoulder with my leg bent upward at the knee, waiting for the groom to take my shin and add the leg hoist to my spring.

When he did clasp my leg, a sudden mysterious warmth seemed to flow from his hand into my flesh, making me keenly aware of him for the first time. When I was seated on the mare's back, his hand remained on my leg, almost caressing. His touch was tender, slow, and deep, the touch of a hand accustomed to gentling animals, a true love touch. I had felt nothing like it since I lost my clan life. I glanced down at him in surprise, just as he raised his eyes to my face. In that instant I felt a shock greater than any yet.

I had seen those eyes before, on a battlefield, in the face of a man dying from my sword-thrust. This man had the same face, the same unusual golden hazel eyes. I could never mistake him. A chill swept over me. Something affected him, too. He stood frozen, his hand still on my leg, our mutual gaze locked onto one another.

For a timeless moment, everything stopped. There was a recognition. Suddenly I was in a different place, under a brighter sun, in a younger age, the noise of battle fading in my ears as I watched those golden eyes calmly regarding the approach of death. His death angel was myself.

Embarrassed by the naked intensity of emotion that flashed between us, I tore my gaze from his and turned Melanie's head toward the open gate. His hand lingered on my leg until the mare stepped away from him. That spot on my shin continued to glow as if sunburned. I looked back only once, as the mare entered a patch of woodland. He was still standing like a statue at the gate, watching me.

The shock of that meeting faded somewhat in the joy of the ride. In every way it was like riding Windeater again. This mare's gaits were the same. She knew me and responded to me with the same gladness. The clear sky, the sharp breeze, the vibrant fall colors added to the ineffable pleasure of moving along with a beloved animal companion—for indeed, between Melanie and me there was an instant love that seemed to have been there always. I think the mare felt it through my body just as I felt it through hers. It was one of the happiest days I had spent in a very long time.

When I returned to the stable, the groom with the golden eyes was nowhere to be seen. Another man, heavyset and black-browed, took Melanie's reins and removed her saddle, dried her back, blanketed her, and led her on a cooling walk. I was glad to see that the Bloodworth grooms took excellent care of their charges.

At dinner, Mattie asked me if I had enjoyed my ride. I was still so euphoric that I could hardly speak, but I said, "I will never, never forget it. It was one of my life's happiest moments."

Mattie smiled. "Then it confirmed your impression that our little Melanie is very like your Windeater?"

"My impression really is that they are one and the same, impossible as that may sound."

We talked of the differences between ancient and modern customs of horsemanship, including the invention of stirrups, which Mattie claimed made riding easier. That reminded me of the groom. "Who is the fellow with yellowish eyes, good-looking, wears a big slouch hat?"

"You must mean Adam," Mattie said. "He's rather new. Have you any criticism of his service?"

"Oh, no," I said. "Everything was fine. I just wondered who he is."

I saw Diana watching me over her glasses with a speculative expression. She knew something unusual had happened in which this man was involved. Soon I would have to tell her about it.

"Adam's case is rather sad, actually," Mattie said. "He's the son of an old friend of mine, who died ten years ago. Adam was left an orphan but a very wealthy one. Unfortunately he was unable to handle the responsibility of a large estate. In just a few years he managed to spend it all on jet-set living, gambling, women, drugs, booze. He went broke and sort of hit bottom.

"Last year be became involved with some kind of fundamentalist cult that seems to have turned him around. He dried out. He joined Alcoholics Anonymous. He's still a bit shaky, but when he came to me looking for a job, I hired him for the sake of my old friend. He's good with horses, played a lot of polo once. He said he didn't want any heavy responsibility, just a quiet life with animals. At least he now has an income and a place to live. He goes to that funny church of his, several times a week, I believe. He keeps to himself and does his job. Where he will go from here I don't know, but for the moment he is in retreat from the world and going through some sort of healing process."

Later, I told Diana about the resemblance between Adam and the man I had killed in battle, without mentioning the strange attraction that I felt for him. Diana said, "Ann, it's been a long time. Perhaps you forget exactly what that fellow looked like."

"Never," I said.

"All right. But it's odd that you should be seeing such resemblances all at once. First the horse, now the man."

"Yes," I said. "It's very odd."

So we left it at that.

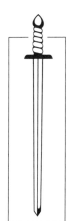

CHAPTER 9

THE NEXT MORNING I WENT AGAIN TO THE STABLE FOR another outing with Melanie. Mattie told me that the mare would be ready for me promptly at eight o'clock. I didn't know whether I should wait for the guidance of Rose or some other servant. I was awake and dressed before dawn, watching the tender colors grow in the sky, feeling restless as one does in a strange place where everyone else is sleeping. I wanted to be outdoors. At seven-thirty I decided to go to the stable alone.

I retraced the route Rose had shown me and quietly let myself out the side door. I breathed deeply as I walked along the dew-wet gravel path, finding in the crisp air a taste almost as sweet as the air of my motherland. Or was I beginning to forget the taste of really pure air?

Melanie was standing cross-tied in the stable, the yellow-eyed groom Adam using a handful of wool to put a final polish on her well-curried coat. He gave a galvanic start when he saw me enter. "Ma'am, you're early," he said. "She's not quite ready."

"That's all right. Take your time. I just felt like enjoying the morning." I stroked the mare's nose. Adam ducked his head. It was almost painfully obvious that we were reluctant to look at each other.

After a few awkward moments I cleared my throat and remarked, "I understand that you have worked here only a short while. Where were you before?"

He didn't answer right away, giving me plenty of time to accuse myself once again of tactlessness, of misunderstanding the conversational rules. Perhaps one did not ask such questions.

Then he said, "I was dead."

A shock went through me. "Dead," he repeated. "And now I'm born again."

"What do you mean?"

"I mean I was dead inside. A lost soul. A bum. I had no job, no family, no hope. Then I found Jesus and was born again. This is my new life."

He looked up and met my gaze for the first time since yesterday. Then I saw the gold Jesus cross hanging at his throat. Diana had told me about this curious symbol, representing the death decreed by the father-god for his so-called son. It was like the gruesome springtime custom of the Greeks, to sacrifice a man, usually called son of the sun, so that his blood shed in agony would nourish the cruel father and maintain his light, inducing him to forgive the sins of men. The Greeks also believed that drinking the victim's blood would help them become godlike and gain immortality. My people knew it was a false, brutal imitation of the real blood of life, which belonged to women and was shed by them without hurt. Yet this unnatural religion, apparently, had prevailed.

"Do you know Jesus?" Adam asked.

"No."

Impulsively he reached forward as if to take my hand, then thought better of it. "Excuse me, but I could help you be saved, as someone helped me. I can see that you are a fine person. I can tell from the way people are with animals. I love animals, even though God didn't give them any souls. You're a fine person and a great horsewoman. It would be a pity if you were not saved."

"Saved from what?" I asked.

"Why—from sin, from death."

"Do you mean that people who know Jesus will not die?"

"Not exactly. They die in the physical sense. But their souls live forever."

"And the others? What happens to their souls?"

"They will suffer."

"Forever?"

"Yes."

"Then their souls are just as immortal as the saved ones, aren't they?"

"Well, I guess so."

During this exchange, Adam and I slowly moved closer to one another, as if drawn like iron and lodestone. Our bodies were speaking an altogether different language. When the space between us narrowed to a few feet, we stopped, gazing steadily into each other's eyes. There was a long silence. I could feel the current passing between us: deep-buried knowledge, memory, recognition, enmity, and something else.

I reached out and placed my hands firmly on his hips. He gasped, shuddered, and rolled his eyes shut. His hands seized my forearms to push me away, then stopped pushing. I felt again that spreading warmth from his touch. Again I was reminded of the long, dry time in which I had felt no human touch of such sensual power.

"This is wrong," he said thickly, wrenching away from me. He took Melanie's little saddle, still stirrupless, and laid it over her back.

I placed myself close behind his shoulder. "Saddle another horse and come with me," I said. "I'd like company on my ride. You can show me the best paths."

He said nothing, but I saw him nod. His cheek was very red.

Soon we went together out into the dewy morning. He rode a rangy bay gelding. He was a competent rider—not expert, but

103

competent. As we rode, he told me that he had once owned some polo ponies, before he ruined himself and lost all his property through sinful living. He loosened up and began to lay aside his diffidence. He told me that I was the most beautiful visitor the Bloodworth estate had ever seen. I would have scorned this as the usual silly lie that men tell women in this country, but I sensed that he was unusually sincere. His golden eyes watched me every moment.

All the while, I was seeing that other face: the dying Greek, the enemy I had unwillingly admired and pitied. I wondered whether Adam had any hint of that scene in his mind. Certainly his attitude toward me was ambivalent. And mine toward him—for, despite my numerous good reasons to avoid him, I felt an overwhelming sexual attraction. For the first time in almost two years I was nearly suffocated with desire for a man.

On this day, according to the ancient tradition, the dead could return to encounter the living. For me it was true. Here I was, riding the mare I had killed in mercy, lusting after the man I had killed in rage, who had been born again. I thought the Mother must have been giving me Her most ironic smile.

So palpable was the sexual heat between us that I was sure Adam would fall into my arms the moment we dismounted in some private place. I chose a sunny little meadow by a stream, where the grass was still growing green and lush. There I halted and slid from the mare's back. Adam followed suit almost immediately, taking the reins of both horses to secure them to a tree. As he did so, I stepped behind him and put my arms around his waist to reach down between his legs.

His penis responded at once, but, as with Jeff, the rest of his body stiffened also. He stood rigid in my embrace for a few minutes, then suddenly turned around and hugged me tightly, running his mouth all over my face in a rather frantic way. His erection drove into my crotch. I was gasping and laughing, ready for a ravenous lovemaking. Then, suddenly, unexpectedly, he shoved me away and covered his face with his hands.

"What's the matter?" I asked.

"I can't, I can't," he moaned. "I made a vow. I am on a mission. You mustn't tempt me anymore."

"What kind of mission?"

"I can't tell you, but I will give you a warning. Beware of Madáme. It has come to the attention of my church that she is a woman of Satan, a witch. She has filled her house with devilish idols. She is planning to challenge God, to lure innocent women away from him."

"Surely you're mistaken," I said. "That's nonsense. She has only collected ancient Goddess figures. She plans to build a temple for women. There's nothing devilish about that."

"The Bible says all female deities are devils," he insisted, "like Ashtoreth, the goddess called 'abomination.' You can read it for yourself. Please believe me. You are too beautiful to be entrapped by witchcraft."

Hoping to change the subject lightly, I smiled. "And you," I said, "are too sexy to worry your head about devils when your body is telling you the truth about life and joy. Just for now, listen to your body." I reached for him again. He allowed me to stroke him, his eyes tightly shut and an expression of near-agony on his face. I opened his shirt and laid my cheek against his chest. His skin smelled subtly sweet, like horse skin. I opened my own shirt and rubbed my breasts against him. I had learned that the men in this world were as responsive to breasts as babies. Perhaps they were perpetually hungry babies.

Again he seized me with wild passion, and for a moment he was all over me, pushing aside my clothes, devouring my body with his hands. I knew by his touch that he would be a good lover if only his strange convictions would permit him. I worked at opening his pants and nearly had his penis in my hand when he pushed me away once more. He went to the stream and fell on his knees, splashing cold water on his face. He clutched his Jesus cross.

"Help me, Jesus," he cried. "Let this cup pass from me."

Half naked, panting, hot-cheeked, I stood over him. "Why do you deny yourself?" I asked. "Look, here I am, ready to give you a taste of the divine. Why don't you want me?"

"I do want you, more than anything," he groaned. "I don't have to tell you that. They warned me that temptation can be almost more than a man can bear. I begin to see that you are one of Madáme's creatures after all, sent to destroy my mission and my soul. In the name of whatever humanness you have, please leave me alone. Whatever the cost, I must do what I was sent to do."

Suddenly I felt chilly. "What were you sent to do?"

He didn't answer. He stood up, buckled his belt, buttoned his shirt, and untied his horse. "For what it's worth to you, you didn't fail," he said. "My desire for you will be with me as long as I live. Good-bye." He mounted and rode away.

I sat down, puzzled. With the vision of him in my mind's eye and the smell of him in my nostrils, I masturbated myself into some semblance of calm. Then I continued my ride. I felt that I had been warned of something very dangerous, and it was not Madáme.

When I returned to the stable, Adam was not there. Melanie was cared for by still another groom, a red-haired, freckle-faced youth. Later that day, as I sat with Mattie and Diana over the temple plans, I asked Mattie if she was aware of Adam's reactionary beliefs.

"I know his church is one of the Jesus-freak variety," she said. "They're very superstitious and naive but probably harmless enough. And they've done Adam good."

"Mattie, I think he is not harmless. I think he's a little crazy, and he means to do you harm." I told her what Adam had said about her "witchcraft" and his "mission." I urged her to dismiss him from her employment before he became violent.

Mattie smiled and said she would think about it. A few minutes later we had become so caught up in the temple project that all else was forgotten.

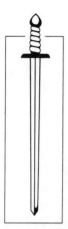

CHAPTER 10

MATTIE'S HALLOWS' EVE RITUAL WAS INTENSELY INTER-esting to both Diana and me. Neither of us had known that beneath the surface of this male-centered culture, groups of women were seeking to recreate the worship of the Mother.

In one way it was an encouraging revelation. In another way it was discouraging to realize that such rituals were made possible only by and for an enlightened minority and were still unknown to—or shunned by—the majority of women. Apparently, many women feared to renounce the cruel motherless god who had cursed them and whose priesthoods had persecuted them through many centuries. They were trained to entrust their spirituality to that god only, despite the absurdities of his theology and the brutalities of his history.

The women who gathered at Mattie's house that night, however, were of a different stripe. There were thirty-seven of them, a number of great mystical power according to the priestesses of my own people. Diana and I made thirty-nine, triple the Mother's sacred thirteen, the number blessed by Her annual moon phases. As Mattie said, what better number to express the Triple Goddess?

Rose came to our rooms with voluminous, ankle-length black silk robes for us to wear to the ceremony. She wore an identical robe, with a silver pentacle on a chain around her neck. She led us to the black door between the colossal Goddesses. The door stood open. Beyond it lay a short passageway lined with glass cases containing books, Goddess figurines, and a large assortment of natural crystals and stones. At the other end of the passageway, another black-robed woman stood before a closed door, holding a lighted candle in her hand.

Rose halted before this woman and performed a ritual gesture, touching her own forehead, left breast, right shoulder, left shoulder, right breast, and forehead again, tracing the pentacle over her heart. The woman responded with the same gesture. Then she opened the door, ushered us in, and, following us, closed the door behind us.

We stood in a large, high-ceilinged room whose walls were covered by long black velvet curtains, in an atmosphere suffused with slow, quiet music and the rich scent of incense. In the center of the room stood a knee-high round table of polished black stone, bearing thirteen black candles in star-shaped holders. At the table's center was a triangular stand holding a large transparent globe, made not of glass but of natural quartz, as I could see from the faint swirls and veilings of white in its depths. Other items scattered on the table included bunches of herbs, sticks, knives, photographs, several pieces of jewelry, a doll, a carved wooden owl, a skull, a fan of figured cards, two ornate silver cups, and the ancient sword from Mattie's collection that so resembled mine.

The warm glow of the candles illuminated the faces of thirty-five women sitting in a circle around the central table, each dressed in a black silk robe with a pentacle amulet. Each woman sat cross-legged on a black velvet floor cushion with an upright back support. Four of these seats were still unoccupied: one to each side of Mattie and two halfway around the circle, where Rose and the doorwoman sat down. Diana and I silently took our places on the other two seats.

The women sat quietly, listening to the music. Some had their eyes closed. Looking around the circle, I saw that besides Rose there were a few others whom I had previously noticed among Mattie's servants. Some of the heads were white or gray with age. Others were younger.

After a while, four women got up. From the altar table one woman took a cup, one a candle, one a bunch of herbs, and one a knife. They carried these items outside the circle, one woman facing each of the four walls. The one bearing the cup spoke first.

"I call upon the Goddess in the South, great virgin and mistress of birth, queen of the blue waters, pearl of the sea, lady of tender love and kindness. Sweet Mother, be with us and bless our circle. Blessed be."

All the women echoed, "Blessed be."

Then spoke the woman with the candle. "I call upon the Goddess in the West, great lover and mistress of passions, queen of red fires, heart of the flame, lady of fierce joy and power. Brilliant Mother, be with us and bless our circle. Blessed be."

Again the women echoed, "Blessed be."

Then spoke the woman with the herbs. "I call upon the Goddess in the North, great giver and mistress of all bounty, queen of the green and golden land, spirit of the earth, lady of planetary cycles. Strong Mother, be with us and bless our circle. Blessed be."

They said again, "Blessed be."

Then spoke the woman with the knife. "I call upon the Goddess in the East, great destroyer and mistress of all gods, queen of the silver air, ruler of souls, lady of death and rebirth. Dread Mother, be with us and bless our circle. Blessed be."

And the chorus said, "Blessed be."

The four women returned the objects to the altar and resumed their places. Mattie took the other cup and turned toward me. The cup contained a red liquid that my nose identified as wine. Mattie dipped her finger in it and traced a crescent on my forehead with her wet finger.

"I, Matilda, bless you, Ann," she said. "Thou art Goddess." Then she gave me the cup, indicating that I should repeat the blessing for the next woman, who turned toward me expectantly and spoke her name, Edith.

"I, Ann, bless you, Edith," I said. "Thou art Goddess." Then I handed the cup to her. It passed on around the circle from woman to woman in the same manner. Tears came to my eyes as I remembered my clansisters' most sacred, secret ritual, performed at the beginning of each year. We blessed one another by touching our foreheads with our own holy moonblood, the real wine of life, visible affirmation of the Goddess spirit within us. The ceremony confirmed our mutual duty to energize and support one another's lives. How could these women here, knowing nothing of my people, have developed a ceremony so similar? Did the true inspiration of the Mother dwell here still, in this dark, hidden room?

When the cup returned to Mattie, she set it down again on the altar, cleared her throat, and addressed the group.

"Dear sisters," she said, "we are gathered on this mystic night to honor the dead, who have passed before us into that eternal cauldron of the elements, from which we all come and to which we all return. Like our foremothers through the centuries, sitting together, we invoke the spirits of our dead and tell their stories. Let the memento mori inspire us."

Across the circle, Rose reached out, took the skull from the altar, and raised it on her hands. She said, "Hecate, Queen of the Dead, hear our rememberings. Cerridwen, Grave-Mother, keeper of the Cauldron of Inspiration, give us true speech. Nephthys, Virgin of the Tomb, be with us in the hour of our own deaths. Ishtar of the Seven Veils, show us the path of the underworld."

She sat back, placed the skull in her lap, took a pearl necklace from the altar, and held it up. This, she said, was her grandfather's wedding gift to her grandmother. It was the only personal gift he ever gave her. For the rest of her life, Rose's grandmother had received only household articles as gifts—kitchen utensils, linens, dishes, brooms, mops. She had been sold into marriage by her father when she was fifteen. Her husband, obtained through some functionary known as a marriage broker, was forty-two and a brute.

Rose said she could still remember her grandfather's harshness toward his wife. The old woman used to cry secretly in the kitchen while cooking, fearing that her husband would dislike the meal and would beat her with his cane. He lived to the age of ninety-three and became ever harder to please as he grew older. The grandmother never defied him, never fought back. But when he died, Rose said, she spat into his coffin and cursed his soul. "Now at last I am free," she said to her children.

When the story was finished, Rose passed the skull to her neighbor, a frail, elderly woman with steel-rimmed eyeglasses. The woman's hands trembled with weakness, but her voice was clear. She said, "Soon I will be among the dead myself. The Crone's hand is on me. I am devoured within by a cancer. I don't complain. My life has been long and interesting. I will end it myself, before I face excessive suffering. Dear Mattie has helped me prepare for that. Tonight I want to tell the story of another suicide, who was always one of my historical heroines. She was Boadicea or Boudicca, a British queen who lived more than two thousand years ago. She led her Goddess-worshiping people in a revolt against the cruel god-worshiping invaders from Rome. Her armies killed more than seventy thousand invaders, but the Romans sent reinforcements in overwhelming numbers until the revolt was crushed. Boadicea's people were destroyed. She killed herself before she could be captured and humiliated. She was a great warrior and she died with dignity. So will I."

I found this account very moving. My eyes stung with tears for this brave old woman, who now passed the skull to her neighbor, a plump middle-aged woman with golden hair. She gave a brief biography of a female writer who had lived thirty years before and produced books that denounced patriarchal religion, explaining how Goddess traditions had been fraudulently concealed or converted throughout history. "Her books were the inspiration of my life," said the golden-haired one. She took a piece of paper from the altar and read to the circle some sentences from those books. They were bold and inspiring words.

The next woman to receive the skull invoked the spirit of her own daughter, killed when her car was hit by another car, driven by a drunken man. The mother showed her daughter's photograph and described her personality. She had been a sweet-natured, cheerful girl with a quick sense of humor. The doll on the altar had been hers when she was very young. The mother missed her unbearably. She wept, and some of the other women wept with her.

The next woman held the skull until the bereaved mother was calm again, then told of a woman named Margaret Sanger, who had fought her country's laws to help women control the number of their children. Before Margaret's time, men were allowed to empty their seed at will into their wives' bodies regardless of the wives' wishes, feelings, or sexual needs. Many women were kept joylessly and continuously pregnant like brood cows. This had gone on even when women were exhausted or sick, or when they were raped or unmarried or too young to be mothers. They were not allowed to prevent or to terminate pregnancies that would disgrace them or cause them to be regarded as criminals, or even pregnancies that might kill them because of the weakness of their bodies.

For years, Margaret was foully persecuted for interfering with this ruthless system, but eventually she won and attained legal sanctions for birth control. Even so, certain religious groups continued to forbid its use to their women members. Margaret, however, had taken the first step toward women's control over their own reproductive organs.

Knowing that I must not speak unless I held the skull, I agreed silently that this Margaret was a heroine indeed.

The skull went on around. Each woman had a story to tell. One gave a brief biography of a great queen named Elizabeth who had lived centuries ago. One told of an ancient priestess-poetess, Velleda, whose works celebrated the Goddess and for that reason were banned by the god's priests. One told of a brilliant woman scientist who had discovered the composition of stars; her work was first disdained and then preempted by her male colleagues, who had fewer qualifications but were paid twice as much money as she. One told of her friend, a nurse who had died of a lung disease that she had caught while tending people already sick with it. The nurse's pin rested on the altar.

When the skull came to Diana, she said, "The dead female I would like to honor tonight is not a human female but a horse, Ann's beloved mare Windeater, who is certainly dead. Yet Ann believes she has found the spirit of Windeater alive again in the body of an animal here on this property. If we speak of the crack between the worlds and of communication between the dead and the living on this Eve of Souls, then surely this strange circumstance is worth mentioning in this circle."

Mattie spoke next about her elder sister Lillian, a free spirit who had renounced the family fortunes and had gone away to live among primitive people on a remote island in the great sea. She fell in love with a tribal chief's son and made her home with him, until she died of a tropical disease. Mattie said that in her childhood she had looked up to Sister Lillian and had longed to emulate her fierce independence. On the altar Mattie had placed a ruby ring that once belonged to her sister. She had given the ring to Mattie on the day of her departure, saying that for the rest of her life she would have no further use for rubies.

Then it was my turn. I took the skull and pressed it between my hands, trying to let my inner vision clothe that bony face with flesh again, to imagine how it looked in life. It was a woman's skull, as shown by the relatively delicate jaw and the domed forehead. For a brief, flickering instant I saw her face, like a shadow over the bone: dark eyes, a long nose, generous easy-smiling lips. "I see her," I said. "She was not very old. I think she died suddenly or violently." I described her. What I did not say was that the face looked very much like my Aunt Leukippe.

The skull went on its way until each woman had told her story and invoked the dead. One that particularly horrified me was an invocation of the collective spirit of "the nine million." It seemed that this was a reference to an estimated nine million innocent women who had been burned alive by priests of the official god in a persecution that had ended only four centuries ago. All of them had been accused of impossible crimes, supposedly engineered by magic and devil worship, and had been forced to confess to these crimes by means of unbearable tortures. And this was the same god to whom most women were taught to pray in these times!

I could hardly believe it. Nine million! Nine times a thousand thousand! A number that boggled the mind, far more women than had ever lived in my country. Yet even those who knew about the persecution of the nine million often seemed willing to forgive the god who had commanded it, even as they forgave him for commanding the torture and murder of his son. No woman of my people would ever have forgiven such things.

Mattie directed us to join hands around the circle and picture all of the invoked dead standing behind us, conscious of our attention on them. I remembered my mother invoking the ancestresses in just this way, during the family circles held at planting and harvest times.

I sat with my eyes closed, striving to feel the presences. Suddenly I did feel something: a touch on the shoulder. Those on either side of me had not touched me; I still held their hands. I opened my eyes and looked behind. No one was there.

The women began a low humming, which seemed to come spontaneously from everyone and no one. The sound gradually rose in volume and pitch, until all the voices were joined in a full-throated cry, like some of the priestess songs that I had once heard in my Mother temple. As the sound continued, the joined hands slowly lifted above the women's heads. Someone shrilled, "Thus we build our temple!" Others made it into a chant. Little by little, the chant died away into silence. All the women leaned forward and placed their hands on the black altar.

This was the end of the solemn part of the ceremony. The skull was returned to the altar, and the comical little wooden owl took its place, being passed from hand to hand. Each one who held the owl talked informally of anything that was on her mind, while all the others listened attentively. No one spoke out of turn. My clansisters had done the same thing when there was a problem to be solved or an accusation to be judged, but the object we had passed among us was a sacred stone. As in the custom of my clansisters, any speaker wishing an immediate response from another person could pass the owl directly to her, after which it would return to the original speaker and continue around the circle. In this way, the terminally ill woman was able to ask for a response from me. She said, "We are happy to have Diana and Ann in our circle tonight. Nearly all of us have read Diana's book and have wanted to meet her. Now I have a request. I wish Ann would tell us something about her own image of the Crone Goddess celebrated at this season. We are fairly sure about her image of the green-robed, flower-decked

116

Maiden celebrated on May Eve in the spring, and we have strong impressions of the fertile Harvest Mother celebrated at Lammas or Lugnasad; but we aren't sure about the Crone of oncoming winter. Sometimes She seems too harsh, cold, or deadly. If you can, Ann, would you tell us about Her?"

I thought carefully and then answered, "The Crone is that part of the Goddess sometimes named Fate or Mother Death. You're right in saying that She often appears ugly, because people see death as ugly—although, in this land, the dying of summer is beautiful, full of bright banners, like a carnival. The priests of your country deny death and say you can live forever, but the truth is that they don't know. My people would consider them foolish. Our priestesses say that Mother Death is the great womb in which everything melts together and is always reformed, you understand? No single individual ever remains, but the Crone makes an infinity of new combinations.

"Without Her, nothing could live, because all living forms must destroy other forms in order to stay alive. A plant may be transformed into the flesh of a cow or a human; cow flesh can also become human flesh if the cow is eaten. The bodies of both animals and humans can return to the soil to grow more plants. Dead flesh can become worms returning to the soil or gases returning to the air. That is why parts of our forebears are always around us, possibly in the very air we breathe and the food we eat. All life past and present is one, ever changing but the same in essence. Birth and death are equally natural and equally sacred, the two ends of each lifetime.

"Our priestesses say that you can't know the Goddess fully until the veil of death is lifted for you, and you look unafraid upon the face that petrifies. We are taught not to fear the ultimate revelation of the Crone. Sometimes She is shown as black, because She is final darkness. Sometimes She appears white, as the winter is white when things are cloaked in cold or as the worms of death are white. And the Maiden is also white, because death means a recombination of the elements and sooner or later a new birth.

"We are like the leaves that fall at this time of year. Through them we are shown our fate. No individual leaf will be recreated, but there will be new leaves to carry on the life of the tree. A motherclan is like the tree. One's own life will not continue, but one's substance will be recycled, and living will continue. That is nature's law, and it is enough for us, for we live every second of our lifetimes supported by nature, whether we are aware of it or not.

"The men here are not satisfied with one lifetime, nor do they understand how the holy spirit of Motherhood labors to create and support each precious life. Such men can foolishly waste their own brief consciousness or that of others. They don't value it enough, because they think it will be restored to them after death; but such an idea is against nature. It is not what the Goddess shows us. It would be better for men to love this life while it lasts and then to let it go without regret. I sometimes think they are like scared rabbits, afraid to look into the void, afraid of the dark not-being, afraid to see the face of the Crone. They would even prefer to imagine a hell of eternal pain than to see their perishable little selves disappearing forever into darkness.

"Children fear the dark, but adults should have more courage. Darkness is the womb and the tomb, the beginning and the end. Nothing exists forever, not even the mountains, not even the stars, not even the gods. Early or late, the Crone swallows them all, for She is infinite time. We are all equally subject to Her law of continual recycling. Why should we fear our own passing? We have no more control over that then we had over our birth."

I held up the carved owl. "It is right that you feel the significance of the owl as the wise Crone's sacred bird. So my people perceived it. The owl is the bird of darkness. It knows the night. It kills swiftly. Mother Death sometimes takes the form of this bird, which embodies Her wisdom. Also, its face often looks like the face of a cat, another of Her sacred creatures. But I hold the owl too long. I am preaching a speech. Forgive me." I passed the carving back.

The woman said, "Nothing to forgive. Your insights are very welcome. You are a true priestess."

I felt embarrassed by such acceptance of my inadequate knowledge. I felt that I didn't deserve the honorable title of priestess. I resolved to read more books and learn more about spiritual ideas in general, to train myself to express them more clearly.

The next woman said, "I am always rather comforted as we come into the dark part of the year. For me it is a quiet time, nature's resting period. Spiritually, it means going deeper into one's self, finding one's roots again."

Another said, "All winter I put out food for the wild animals and birds. It makes me feel that I am nature's helper, giving her creatures a little better chance of survival for another year. If I were a woodland priestess like the old Druidesses, I'm sure this would be one of my primary duties."

Another said, "Samhain has always been a special day for me. I like it because I have it to myself, in a way. Few others think of it as an official holiday—holy day, that is. The real meanings of the owls, cats, witches, ghosts, and jack-o'-lanterns have been forgotten. Yet for me it has always been holy. I like the orange and black colors of fire in the night. I like the old connotations of final harvesting, storing supplies, preparing for a long winter sleep. It's a good time, and I'm glad to spend it here with my good sisters."

Rose read a poem that she had recently written. Mattie talked about designs for the temple. Edith spoke of her upcoming trip to a place called Australia—"on the other side of the

119

globe," she said. (I still had difficulty envisioning Mother Earth as a globe, even though it did make symbolic sense.) Diana confessed that when planning this visit, she had not expected to participate in a rich spiritual experience. "It seems so comfortable to be in a circle of women, creating a ritual," she said. She hoped that the projected Goddess temple would provide similar comforts for multitudes of women.

When all had finished speaking, the women joined hands again and chanted their closing chorus:

> By the earth that is Her body,
> By the air that is Her breath,
> By the fire that is Her bright spirit,
> By the living waters of Her womb,
> The circle is open but unbroken.
> The peace of the Goddess go in our hearts,
> Merry meet, and merry part, and merry meet again.
> Blessed be.

Afterward, musical instruments were produced. One woman played a drum, one a flute, one a guitar. Some of the women danced. Others set out plates of food and bottles of wine and juices. Everyone ate and talked. The ceremony became a party, at which Diana and I were guests of honor.

The hour was late when the women said their good nights and went their separate ways. Mattie and the women of her household exchanged hugs. Mattie didn't treat her servants as inferiors. They seemed more like family members. I could understand how Mattie inspired so much goodwill and loyalty in her helpers.

I was conscious of this also on the following morning, when Mattie, Diana, and I met at the breakfast table. The pantry woman and the maid no longer seemed robotlike strangers. We exchanged friendly smiles and greetings, although they served us as quickly, silently, and efficiently as before. More important than such formal designations as host, guest, employer, or employee was our shared womanhood. For the first time since the loss of my motherclan, I felt at home with people other than Diana.

I went to the stable for a farewell look at Melanie. As I was patting her nose and whispering to her, Adam appeared in the doorway. He stopped and stared at me, a shaft of sunlight imparting a topaz glow to his eyes. "You're back," he said. Today there was no "ma'am."

"We're leaving soon," I said. "I wanted to say good-bye to Melanie. And to you."

He took a step backward. "I thought you were innocent and good, a child of God. I was mistaken. Now I see that you're one of them—the witches."

As he said the word *witches* I saw in his mind a collection of evil spirits in women's bodies. Mattie seemed to be a major she-devil, but all of them were commanded by a larger male devil something like our own Horned God of the spring planting. Poor Adam saw male domination even among his imaginary demons. I felt a curious stew of feelings about him; all at the same time, I pitied him, desired him, scorned his wrongheadedness, and longed to enlighten him. Physically I still sensed the powerful attraction between our bodies, more compelling than any I had ever felt before. I know he felt it, too.

"You're wrong about the women," I said. "They do nothing evil. They're good people. They want to nurture and comfort the world that men are injuring."

"They want to deny God, and so do you," he said in a bitter tone.

"I don't know your God, and from what I've heard of him, I think I'd prefer not to know him. But believe me when I say Ms. Bloodworth and her friends don't concern themselves about him one way or another. Come, let's part friends. I bear you no ill will. I think you're beautiful." I held out my hand to him.

He stood still, his throat working as if he were choking on something. Then he seized my hand abruptly and gave it a hard squeeze, staring into my face. For a moment I thought he might throw his arms around me, but he did not. He whirled and hurried away without another word. I well knew at least one component of his agitation, and this made me smile. That was not a final good-bye, I thought. We will meet again because the Mother has decreed it. There is a purpose here, which will be revealed in time.

Before we left, Diana and I promised Mattie that we would return to attend the dedication of her Goddess temple. We said good-bye to Rose and other members of the household and drove away through the tall gates. The guard saluted us.

On the way home, I talked to Diana about Adam. She was unwilling to believe that he actually embodied the man I had killed in battle. "But why not," I asked, "if a living horse can embody my Windeater? Besides, there is a deep hostility of our spirits even though we each feel a hot desire. I don't think he has any sense of a former meeting, but he is afraid of me all the same. I am—what's that term?—under his skin."

Diana laughed. "I'm sure you are," she said, "and I'm sure the poor schlunk won't forget you in a hurry. You don't know what a power you are, Ann. Now let's stop for lunch. How about one of those awful chocolate milkshakes you like so much?"

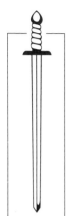

CHAPTER 11

DIANA AND I TRAVELED TOGETHER TO MANY INTER-
views, workshops, lectures, and other public appearances calculated to enhance sales of her book
and my videotape. In these travels I gained some
idea of the enormous size of this land that was considered a single nation, of the diversity of its people, and of both the benefits
and the evils of its culture.

After I had become more accustomed to highways, cities,
and airports, I lost much of my initial enthusiasm for them. I
caught myself in nearly the same state of indifference as my fellow passengers to the extraordinary sights to be seen from airplane windows. Views of the land from high up began to seem
more sad than thrilling. I began to notice vast spreads of poten-
tially good farmland buried under sprawling roads, towns, shopping malls, parking lots, and factories; land poisoned and ruined
by industrial waste; land black with soot or sterilized by
machines. I now saw the ugly gray hue of filthy streams that
had once run clear, the dim brown pall of foul air over every
urban area, and the scars where the earth had been chewed
open. Such sights filled me with cold dread. Surely, I thought,
the Mother must be very angry at children who left canker sores

all over Her body, turned Her breath and lifeblood into poison, and generally behaved like Her disease parasites. These people were making Mother Earth sick, draining Her health away to support their amazing civilization.

As I met and talked to more people, I learned more of the customs and laws of this land. Television showed that the breaking of the law received much attention and television shaped the lives and attitudes of the people. Every person from her or his infancy was given daily television lessons in hurting, shooting, killing, robbing, burning, blowing things up, and abusing others—especially men abusing women. Through television, every child acquired vivid images of a world full of evil human acts, while she or he remained incongruously ignorant of the natural world and of how it might be improved. There were few television lessons in sexual loving, mothering, caring for the sick, tending animals, learning to concentrate, or working the soil.

Children in this society usually remained unaware of the nature of trees, plants, or herbs, of the habits of insects or animals, of the properties of stones, the movements of the stars, or the phases of the moon. They didn't know or care where their daily food came from. They never thought of how the soil grows crops, or of mother cows robbed of the milk that nature had intended for their calves, or mother hens robbed of the eggs that nature meant to nurture chicks, or mother ewes robbed of their lambs who were slaughtered for human food. Despite much freely available information, the children usually knew almost nothing about the workings of their own bodies. They had no patience to watch spiders spinning their webs or birds building their nests, yet they would sit still for hours every day to watch cartoon characters kill each other over and over and to be trained by commercials to desire unwholesome foods and pointless toys.

In schools, children soon learned how to obtain drugs that would dull their minds even more. The drug distribution system was supposedly illegal, but actually it supported a huge segment of the economy. This system could reach every person at an early, formative age. Adult authorities only pretended to prevent this. They shifted responsibility onto the children themselves, whom they counseled to "say no," but all the while, much of the adult population was saying yes and making a profit from drugs and drug-related activities. Children who didn't know how a man should make love to a woman were nevertheless quite familiar with techniques of injecting heroin into a vein; they had seen it done on television.

Matters in the forefront of consciousness for both young and old often seemed of the utmost triviality to me. People knew about things like the personal lives of rock musicians and other entertainers; they knew the repetitive words to popular songs, the latest developments in television soap operas, minute variations in makes of cars, brand names of thousands of consumer products, and the latest fads in dress or hairstyles. While the male-dominated military establishment continued to create and stockpile horrendous weapons capable of killing every form of life including children, humanity's future, this world's women continued to talk together of parties, recipes, floor waxes, and furniture polish.

Apparently it didn't occur to women that they could rise up together in a solid sisterhood and declare in one voice that this world's ways were wrong, that wasting natural resources was a crime, that mind-destroying drugs had to be eliminated from schools, that raping and killing had to be stopped, that men had to take their morality from mothers instead of from fathers. Television incessantly repeated the message that women had to be powerless in the face of male power or that it was "unwomanly" for women to pass judgment on the doings of men. Television never showed women how to rebel.

Along with this trivialization or neglect of women's vital sense of relatedness went an inevitable disintegration of clan and family, so pervasive that it was even regarded as normal. For example, everyone expected teenage children to experience alienation, loneliness, and a degree of hostility toward their elders that would have been unheard of among my people. Everyone expected adult children (even daughters!) to leave their mothers' homes and live far from other family members, to bring up their own children in isolation. Everyone expected to be abandoned by their own children when they grew old and helpless. Elders were isolated in impersonal institutions and faced death alone.

Children rarely had grandmothers to teach and guide them. Television had taken the grandmother's place. The scattering of families was encouraged by employers, who often moved male employees far from their original homes, expecting that each man would drag a wife and children along wherever he went. No one seemed to find this uprooting of families seriously disturbing, except some of the children, whose adjustment problems were not considered important.

From a human viewpoint it was a sad world, full of sad, lost people. Those who were most miserably unhappy were usually taught to blame themselves for their inability to adjust to this maladjusted society. They were taught by special professionals called shrinks, who took a lot of money from the suffering ones but rarely relieved their sufferings.

Observing these things, I thought the real cause of widespread spiritual malaise was the culture's loss of the Mother image, accompanied by disrespect for motherhood in general. These motherless children didn't understand what was happening to them: living with material comforts beyond the grandest dreams of their ancient foremothers, they were starving to death in the midst of a feast.

When spiritually deprived people sought spiritual comfort, they had no choice but to go to male priests who offered only a Father image, claiming that this personage (whose reality could never be questioned) would love and support them. Yet he was also unpredictable, judgmental, implacable, and ferociously punitive. Many believed that he would condemn a majority of people to eternities of unbearable torture. He was opposed to sensual and sexual comfort. He had even made women's birth-giving into a penance for some primordial but unforgotten sin. He was invoked in wars and thanked for victories that killed thousands of innocent women and children. To me he sounded like a very evil god.

I could understand why women like Mattie considered it necessary to establish a Mother temple and begin to instruct people in the proper veneration of the Goddess, not as a transcendent deity but as the life force inherent in nature and especially in women. Followers of the Mother would face no hell, only death and natural recycling—an idea that could eliminate many foolish fears. Followers of the Mother could understand the vital necessity of the blood bond. Followers of the Mother could recognize that most varieties of love between humans were good, not evil, that the physical body should be honored, comforted, pleasured, and healthily maintained, never ne-glected, and that similar care should be extended to the physical body of Mother Earth and all Her creatures.

Into the empty space left by the loss of the Mother had come that deity to whom Adam claimed allegiance: Jesus. It seemed this Jesus was a noticeably feminized man who cured the sick, raised the dead, professed a motherly regard for little children, counseled passive acceptance of blows from one's ene-mies, and allowed himself to be tortured to death, at the father-god's command, a long time ago.

There were radical differences of opinion about this Jesus. Some said he was a man like other men. Some said he was the god himself. Some said he was the god's miraculously begotten child, like those Eastern kings described by our priestesses, born of the priestess-queens who mated with gods on mountaintops.

Still others attributed to Jesus a confusing mixture of mortal and divine natures, not clearly differentiated from the mixture of mortal body and immortal soul that everybody else was supposed to have anyway. Many people still symbolically ingested Jesus, as if to assimilate his qualities into themselves, by eating flour paste and wine that their priests solemnly declared was Jesus' flesh and blood.

In the midst of an astonishing diversity of religious sects and theologies, none of these ideas found universal acceptance, but all were accepted by someone. The general view of Jesus' personality considered him gentle, pacific, loving, accepting, and prone to victimization—in short, motherlike, as mothers were perceived here, in strong contrast to the vengeful god with whom he was also identified.

The mighty power of motherhood was cynically exploited and simultaneously belittled by all-male priesthoods who convinced women that they must subject their children to constant instruction in this all-male religion, on pain of terrible consequences if the children should grow up "irreligious." There was no official alternative to father worship or man worship. Naturally, ecclesiastical fathers insisted that girls as well as boys had to be trained in this unfemale religion, so they would absorb reverence for the male principle with their earliest lessons and learn to enslave themselves to male authority.

If Diana's theory was correct, then the beliefs and customs of the Greeks in my own time had now prevailed completely over the ancient culture of motherclans and the religion of the Goddess. I often thought how discouraged my clansisters would be if they knew that their own beloved faith had no future and that the aggression of father worshipers would eventually destroy our people and our way of life. In vain, it seemed, had our young women and men trained themselves as warriors to fight off the Greek menace. We would lose in the end. Civilization would set an irrevocable course toward the general nastiness of this dim, unloving age.

Sometimes I cursed the fate that had mysteriously catapulted me into this unwanted knowledge and abandoned me in this unnatural world. I was sustained only by Diana's unfailing kindness and by the memory of Mattie's purpose. The women of Mattie's group seemed almost the only truly enlightened people I had met.

Certainly we met some abysmally unenlightened people, some of them very hostile to our message. Some of our interviewers publicly mocked us; others insulted or berated us. Religious types invariably declared us evil in one way or another. Much was written about us, the more intelligent authors pointing out the improbability of Diana's theory about me, the less intelligent ones simply declaring us atheists, troublemakers, witches, demonesses, or radical feminists, all of which terms seemed more or less interchangeable in their minds.

We were often accused of deliberate fraud. Sometimes I was regarded as the deceiver, with Diana as my dupe. Sometimes it was the other way around: I was viewed as a simpleminded musclewoman hypnotized by Diana into believing in a past life. Sometimes we were called a pair of con artists who had jointly cooked up a fantastic scam.

There were also many who believed us. Some of the people who interviewed us were courteous and serious, not slyly aggressive like Billy Bobb. Both women and men who came to our lectures frequently asked honest questions, to which we tried to give honest answers.

One of those honest answers brought on another notorious incident. We were on a television talk show with a male interviewer, taking questions from members of the audience. I had learned that such questions were usually prescreened by the program directors, so everyone knew in advance what would be said and who would say it. But sometimes, if she had the chance, Diana would recognize an unscheduled participant. On this day we had a little time to spare. Diana called on a woman wearing dark glasses and a large flesh-colored bandage across her nose.

The woman stood and addressed herself to me. "I don't know if you remember, but we met once before," she said. "Several years ago in a parking lot, you defended me against my brute of a husband. We're separated now and I've filed for divorce, but my husband won't stay away from me. He claims we're still married, and he has a right to live in my house and sleep in my bed. He shows up every couple of weeks and I can't keep him out. He's still a brute. I've called the police again and again. They can't seem to keep him restrained. Lately he hit me with a poker and broke my nose." She removed her dark glasses and showed purple-black bruises around both eyes. I recognized her as the woman with the groceries, whose husband had been slapping her and her children.

"Ann, I didn't know who you were, that time," she went on, "but I've followed all the news about you since the book came out. My question is this. What did women in your country do about abusive husbands? If a man chose to hit his wife, since he was generally stronger, how did you stop him?"

"In the first place," I answered, "my clan would have thought it highly abnormal for members of the same family to strike one another in anger. Our children were taught not to express anger in that way, just as your children are taught not to defecate in public. It wasn't done by sane people, though sometimes it might have been done by those who were hopelessly deviant. I never heard of such an occurrence in my village."

"But if it did occur, would you have a rule for handling it?"

"Yes. The Mother gave laws to cover everything. If a man should use a stick, stone, blade, or any other weapon with intent to injure a woman or a child, then the hand that held the weapon must be chopped off at his wrist."

The audience gasped. The interviewer said, "Well, Ann, that does seem a bit harsh for such a gentle, peaceable society as you claim to describe. How would you justify such extreme punishment?"

"It only seems extreme to those who are used to the idea of men hitting women," I said. "Actually it would inflict less pain than a beaten wife suffers through many repeated hurts. The Mother provided punishment to fit this crime, which was rare among us, as rare as rape, which was also nearly unthinkable. Diana has already written how our law dealt with rapists."

The interviewer gave a somewhat theatrical shudder. "Yes, I guess we all know about that, but we probably wouldn't want to discuss it in front of the camera. How would you deal with a man who used only his fists as weapons against women?"

"He would lose a finger for each repetition of the offense, because fingers close up into fists."

The woman with the dark glasses was now sitting down, and another person was standing and asking something. I tried to concentrate on subsequent answers, but that woman's battered face continued to haunt me. Three weeks later I found out why.

We were in yet another hotel room. Diana came in with the morning newspaper. The same woman's picture was there, nose bandage and all. The headline said, "Woman Amputates Estranged Husband's Hand," followed by, "Cites Amazon's Advice." The story said Irma Ledburn's estranged husband had forced his way into her apartment and demanded a dinner, which she gave him, including wine laced with sleeping pills. While he slept, she used a hatchet to cut his hand off. She then called an ambulance to take him to the hospital. She told police that she had endured years of torment from this man without effective protection, so she had resorted to the Amazon law as elucidated by me. Diana's book, my tape, and the relevant interview show were mentioned.

The story received much publicity. Feminist groups took up Irma Ledburn's cause and marched in front of the courthouse at her trial, protesting that her willful injury of her husband was much less than his willful injuries of her. Eventually her case was dismissed.

Then it happened again—and again. Suddenly there was a rash of husband mutilations by women who had endured years of battering. Some of the husbands retaliated by mutilating or even murdering their wives. Here and there, female vigilante groups calling themselves Amazons began to punish abusive men with more "behandings," as the press styled them. Some of these groups also castrated convicted rapists. The general violence was horrifying. I was appalled by the cruelty that lurked beneath the surface of this society, ready to burst forth at the slightest word.

Worst of all, nearly every news story traced the violence back to me and that fateful interview. I was portrayed as a sadistic man-hater as well as a fraud or a dupe. I was ridiculed for representing cruel punishments as the normal routines of an allegedly gentle society. No one noticed my reference to the extreme rarity of such punishments or the horror that they justly inspired.

Diana and I received a lot of hate mail. A man addressed me as "the loony fucking cock-docking bitch" and wrote that I should have my hair set on fire, my feet shredded, and my tits cut off and stuffed down my throat. He signed himself "a good God-fearing Christian, like you don't believe in." Women called me a benighted savage. One said I should be kept in a cage until I found God. Another declared that the devil would come and get me at the dark of the moon in exactly two months' time.

There was a distressed—and distressing—letter from a woman who plaintively asked, "Why can't you keep your sick, sadistic fantasies to yourself? Don't you know we mothers already have too much ugly violence in the media to keep our children safe in an unsafe world? People like you want to repay violence with more violence, like revenge and war. You give us no solution but only one more version of the problem."

That one made me cry, because she was right. By telling the truth and being myself, a warrior, I had in effect promoted one more idea of cruel behavior. I couldn't have known how eagerly people would act on it, but I saw that my words had made bad situations worse. Now, when Diana and I gave lectures, there was always some braying male voice on the periphery, heckling us about behandings.

Then came the Sarah Fine article. Six months after the interview, a magazine article by Sarah Fine presented the results of some research. She concluded that the nationwide incidence of wife battering had indeed declined since the behandings had occurred. Also, there were fewer rapes reported than in any of the previous five years. Sarah Fine suggested that since violent men understood and responded to violence, they could only be motivated by fear. Cruel retaliation by women actually functioned as a deterrent, because it gave male bullies some reason to fear women. Sarah Fine cited several instances of abused wives who had contacted "Amazon" groups, who in turn had issued warnings to the abusive husbands. Often, the wife beating had stopped. Other examples were reported of women who prevented rape by threatening the would-be rapist with "Amazonian" retribution. This approach seemed to be working better than the ponderous traditional mechanisms of law enforcement. The article was widely circulated and reprinted. Diana was so pleased that she sent a congratulatory letter to Sarah Fine.

Unfortunately, we found that fear could also drive certain antifeminist fanatics to the brink of lunacy. Late one winter evening, Diana and I were leaving a television studio, crossing the sidewalk toward a waiting car. A thin cold drizzle was falling. Clusters of people stood under their umbrellas. Colored light from shop windows made a rainbow glow on the slick street. Escorted by studio guards, we were only a few steps from the car when a shot was fired. Diana suddenly fell backward. People shrieked.

I looked in the direction of the shot and saw a man in a dark overcoat, still holding up a pistol in both his hands. He cried, "Die, Amazon bitch!" Shoving my way between umbrellas and people who were standing as if paralyzed, I leapt at the man. He stepped backward, angled the gun toward me, and fired again. He missed. There was another outcry from the crowd, which was disintegrating as people fled in all directions.

Eyes wide with panic, the attacker threw his gun at me and turned to run away. No doubt it was his panic that saved my life. Had he kept his head and shot at me again, with good aim, he could hardly have missed. I was almost on him. The gun struck me on the rib cage, the blow softened by my heavy coat. It hurt but did not slow me down. Before the man had run three steps, I grabbed him by the collar. I pulled him off balance, kicked his feet out from under him, and chopped at his neck as he went down. I was feeling an intense regret that my sword was not at my belt. I wanted to kill this man.

He was struggling, trying to punch me, as I dodged behind his head. I seized his hair and banged his head on the cement until he stopped moving and drops of blood began to fly, with each blow, from a spreading puddle underneath him.

Some people took my arms and raised me up. I tore free of them and went over to Diana. I was relieved to see that she had not been killed. The studio guards were bending over her. One of them had placed a rolled-up coat under her head. Rain was falling on her face. Her eyes were open. She smiled weakly and reached out a hand to me.

As always in the midst of shocking events, it seemed that normal time ceased to exist. I don't know whether it was a long time or a short time before there were screaming sirens and flashing red lights. I crouched on the sidewalk holding Diana's hand. An ambulance came. Men carefully lifted Diana onto a stretcher. Other men lifted the inert attacker onto a similar stretcher and carried him toward the same ambulance.

That galvanized me. "No!" I shouted. "You won't put him next to her!" Ready to fight, I blocked the stretcher bearers' way. A police officer gently took my arm and drew me aside. "Take it easy, he'll be guarded," he said. "We know what he did. You're the woman's friend? Relax. We'll take you to the hospital to see her. We just want to get your statement first."

Bewildered and distracted, I answered the policemen's questions. Then I was driven to the hospital by a stocky, blunt-faced cop with friendly blue eyes. He helped me find Diana and the doctor who examined her. The doctor said that she had been wounded in the shoulder and that it was not serious. She would recover. I saw her, bandaged, sleeping peacefully in a bed. Weak with relief, I let the friendly cop take me back to our hotel.

In a way, this incident was the ultimate revelation to me of the constant threat that simply living in this allegedly civilized world could be. My people feared sudden attacks of evil spirits of disease or misfortune, hard winters, crop failures, epidemics, abnormal births, cradle deaths, accidents, aches and pains. We didn't fear each other. These people faced the possibility of sudden lunatic attacks in every city. Which world had made real progress? I wondered.

Diana's attacker didn't die either. His fractured skull eventually mended, after which he was sent to a hospital for the insane, where he would be relieved of the necessity to work, would be fed and clothed at public expense, and would be tended by shrinks for the rest of his life or until they decided to set him free.

My greatest regret was that I had not killed him.

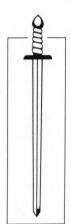

CHAPTER 12

I TENDED DIANA WHILE SHE WAS RECOVERING FROM HER bullet wound, just as she had tended me while I was recovering from mine. After she came home from the hospital, her nephew Jeff visited at intervals to observe her progress. At first he was diffident with me, but as I showed him no sign of either hostility or seductiveness, he was reassured and began to relax. I remained carefully neutral. Eventually we became something like friends.

One afternoon while Diana took her nap, Jeff and I were sitting together over cups of tea. I remarked, "It's amazing, this murderous hate that some of your men seem to hold for women. Where does it come from, Jeff?"

He put down his cup and tented his fingers. I had learned that this gesture was usually intended to signify serious thought. "Psychologists have been studying the problem lately," he said. "The current theory is that woman-hating men — and bullies generally — have been abused as children. In adulthood, they direct their unconscious residues of rage and fear toward those who look unable to fight back. They pick on women for a lot of reasons. First, in childhood they probably resented what they perceived as weakness on the part of their mothers, who were unable to protect themselves or their children from the father's attacks. Second, they wanted to identify with the stronger one: to become the abuser rather than the victim. Third, they are threatened by their own sexual nature, which draws them toward women. They particularly dislike women who seem strong, both because this contradicts their favored stereotype and because they fear that women's resentment of their attitude might explode into fatherlike aggression. Needless to say, they haven't any insight into women's real nature." He gave me a small smile. "We all have a little trouble with that from time to time."

"If all this is understood," I said, "then why is it allowed to go on? Why are men not trained to be kinder fathers?"

"There are old, time-hallowed precedents of male dominance in the family, laid down many centuries ago and reinforced by everything: religion, law, education, social custom, folklore, conventional wisdom—everything. Our laws still recognize a father's control as 'head of household,' and our mores still give him room to be tyrannical if he happens to be that sort of person. There aren't any committees set up to judge fathering behavior."

"The natural way is for women to be the judges," I declared. "Who else knows what is best for children? Who cares more? No one pays as much attention to a child's needs as its mother."

"Usually that's true, but it's not true all the time. Sometimes fathers are kinder than mothers. Sometimes it's the women who brutalize the children."

"Then they have been driven mad by living in conditions that aren't natural," I said, "like mice who eat their own young when they are kept in cages. Still, even in captivity, the Goddess gives nearly every mother a loving heart."

"You might say that civilization is a kind of captivity," he mused. "We're voluntary prisoners, though. Most of us like it. It's comfortable. We don't have to exert ourselves much to get the necessities of life. We become complacent. We men in this society have been complacent for a long time, even when we hurt each other and ourselves."

"Then you do understand," I said.

"Doctors are supposed to understand a lot of things that they really don't know much about. I know I didn't understand women very well, as people, that is. Aunt Di's book was an eye-opener for me. After reading it, I'm getting along better with my wife, my female patients and colleagues, nurses, everybody. Even if it is just a fantasy, that book makes some really useful points."

"You think it is a fantasy?"

"Ann, I don't know. I guess you sincerely believe it. I have to admit that some things are hard to explain away—your sword, your language, your—um—your scars. Maybe the things you have to say can't be said in any other way. Even if you imagined it all, it takes a good imagination to envision a society so alien to ours. After all, even trained anthropologists have trouble getting into the mindset of an unfamiliar culture."

"You think that's true even for a culture that is closer to real nature? One that recognizes the primacy of the mother for humans, just as other creatures recognize it for their own kind?"

"I can't argue the point, Ann. I'm just a simple sawbones. These matters are too deep for me. Everybody has a different answer to the old question, What is truth? For me, truth is thermometers and urinalyses and X rays and what goes on in the physical organism. I know what I know, but even in my own field I often have to guess."

"I know there are many people who don't believe I tell the truth, so they don't pay attention. Tell me, Jeff, what can I do to help women, to help mothers? How can I make a difference here and now, in this world?"

He shrugged. "Beats me. Usually, people who want to make changes in society take up some form of counseling or teaching.

That means you have to go to school, take courses, get certified in a field like psychology or social science. To help women specifically, you might do volunteer work at a rape crisis center or a shelter for battered women. You could even do volunteer work at the hospital."

"In my country, it was the priestesses who gave most help to other women with all kinds of physical, emotional, or spiritual problems."

"Yes, but this isn't that kind of country, Ann."

"There will be at least one Goddess temple, though. Perhaps I can be a priestess there." I told him about Mattie's plan. He listened gravely, but I could tell that he thought the whole idea rather frivolous and cultic, unrelated to what he considered real life.

"Elderly rich people take up all kinds of projects," he said. "That's the way they are. They need to find something to spend their money on before they have to go and leave it behind. No one yet has figured out how to take it along."

"With Mattie, it's more than that," I insisted. "She has a true vision. She knows how women are spiritually impoverished in this country. She sees the need."

"Maybe so," he said, evidently trying to humor me. I could see that he thought the point too trivial or too irrelevant to argue. But I sensed something else beneath the surface of his indifference: an unacknowledged fear. He was wondering what the practical results might be if a Goddess religion became firmly established among the women of this world that had long imagined only a God. How might it change things? Giving the idea his attention even for a few seconds, he sensed that it would mean profound changes. He didn't want to contemplate the possibilities.

This talk with Jeff gave me a deeper understanding of the kinds of resistance that could greet Mattie's temple project. Jeff was no woman-hater. He had no profound intellectual commitment to patriarchy itself. It was just the atmosphere he grew up in and was used to. The idea of a deity had little place in his customary thoughts, but he saw no reason to alter its gender. After all, a male image of the deity did work to some advantage for every man.

That was the obvious reason for men's having created the image in the first place.

As time passed and the Goddess temple took shape, Diana and other journalists published several articles about it. Some people responded with intense curiosity and interest in the subject. Others seemed indifferent or hostile. The topic was usually presented with the catchall modifier, *controversial.* Sometimes the controversy seemed to be about whether Mattie should be allowed to build her temple at all. Some groups wanted it outlawed but couldn't find any legal precedent. It seemed that the country's laws officially promised freedom of religion, although many people hated these laws and behaved as though creeds differing from their own should be mercilessly destroyed.

The building of the Goddess temple encountered a few setbacks based on this unwritten intolerance. Some workers walked off the job, following orders from their own religious leaders. There was petty sabotage. Mattie had commissioned a lovely white marble Goddess statue, ten feet high, to be installed in the sanctuary. One night while it was awaiting final positioning, someone broke into the enclosure, removed its wrappings, and spray-painted its lips, nipples, and yoni a bloody red. Then the vandal wrote "Big Fat Devil Bitch" across its belly. I laughed when I heard this but also felt puzzled. I was never quite sure how the word for a female dog had come to have a pejorative meaning in this society. After all, of all animals the bitch was perhaps friendliest to and most popular among humans. Besides, she was intelligent, trainable, loyal, affectionate, courageous, and an excellent mother to her young—altogether an admirable creature. Could her fall from grace have been related to the fact that ancient priestesses used to call themselves the Mother's bitches?

Fortunately the paint was easily removed from the statue, and there was no further desecration. The incident was attributed to "kids." Surely, I thought, nowhere else in the world was it so taken for granted that children would commit crimes against property and persons. Criminal misbehavior or vandalism seemed to be routinely expected of the young. I wondered if this circumstance might have something to do with the harsh behaviors of fathers that Jeff had described.

A few weeks before the temple's official opening, Mattie again sent us an invitation to her house. The dedication date was set for the first of May, which Diana dated back to ancient festivals in honor of the Goddess in Her springtime guise as the Green Maiden, whom our priestesses used to call Maia. Diana said the night before this festival was known as May Eve, Beltane, or Walpurgisnacht. It had continued to be sacred to certain manifestations of the Goddess even long after patriarchy had presumed to dethrone Her. It was a time for the wearing of the green in honor of the budding and flowering earth and for celebrating fertility. Priestesses of my clan had always taught that the land would not bring forth crops unless the right ceremonies were performed at this crucial time.

I was glad to see the time of year so well chosen. The month of beginnings and burgeonings seemed an ideal time for dedicating a temple. I was excited by the prospect of seeing Melanie again and Adam, whose image appeared in my private sexual fantasies more often than I would have cared to admit. I had taken no lovers for a very long while, but I was annoyed with myself for perversely paying so much attention to the only man who had ever refused me—and to whom I was linked by mysterious and dreadful bonds.

Unfortunately for Diana, it was raining on the twenty-ninth of April, the day set for our journey to Mattie's estate. Although

141

her shoulder had long since healed, Diana still complained of wet-weather aches that made driving uncomfortable for her. The trip delighted me, however. Gray skies gave a misty sweetness to the fresh green on the hills. Trees and young undergrowth seemed to be drinking the rain eagerly, despite the sad fact that the rain was too acid to be good for them. They could not protest, of course; they would quietly continue to put on the hopeful green robes of spring until the time when they would, just as quietly, die.

To me this apocalyptic end seemed remote enough not to spoil the day, just as the knowledge of our own inevitable death does not spoil life's happy moments. Or perhaps I was becoming infected with the same insouciant apathy that governed so much of the behavior of these self-privileged, self-threatened people.

On passing through Mattie's gates, I began to look eagerly for the horses. The pasture, however, was empty. Rose met us at the door of the house.

"How nice to see you again," she said warmly. "Madáme has asked me to settle you in the same rooms you had before. She's busy in her office, but she'll meet you for tea in the library at four o'clock. Meanwhile, make yourselves comfortable."

On the way to our rooms, I asked Rose about the horses. "They're indoors today on account of the wet," she said. "We're trying to keep them clean. If you want to see Melanie, you can go down to the stable any time. There's an umbrella for your use in the closet of your room. Do you remember the way? If not, I will show you."

"I remember, thanks." I didn't want to make it explicit, even to myself, how much I was hoping to see Adam alone. Nevertheless, I felt that odd internal jitter usually described as one's heart beating faster.

I hurried to the stable. I found Melanie in a box stall, calmly munching her hay. She looked up, nickered in surprise, and swung toward me as I entered. She knew me. She lipped my hair as I hugged her strong, silky neck. We were like close friends after a separation, glad to see one another. How could it be that this mare and I had met only once before in this life?

I spent a half hour talking to Melanie in the warm, rustling, hay-scented peace of the barn, to the accompaniment of gentle spring rain on the roof. I didn't see Adam. Another groom came along to muck out a nearby stall. I asked him where Adam was.

"That one was let go," he said.

"You mean he was fired? Why?"

"Don't rightly know." I could tell that he knew very precisely. "Somebody said he was rude to one of Madáme's guests or something. He was an OK worker. Good with the horses."

"He was fired for rudeness?" I repeated, surprised.

"Can't rightly tell, ma'am. You ask Miz Bloodworth about it."

"All right. Thank you."

The man lowered his head and resumed his chore.

Later, over tea in the library, I did ask Mattie about it. She placed the delicate porcelain cup gently down in its saucer and drew a deep breath. Her expression was melancholy.

"Suddenly, one day, he attacked Glinda," said Mattie. "Glinda Rivall, the actress. She was here for a weekend. Let's see, it must have been more than a year ago. Yes, shortly after your visit. The man intruded on her private ritual at the woods altar. Instead of going about his business, he called her a limb of Satan and attacked her with a stick. She was quite bruised, poor dear. I remember her sitting at dinner with a black eye. Of course Adam was dismissed immediately. I suppose he was crazy. So much for the beneficial results of religious fundamentalism. The kind of help he needs, I can't provide."

I exchanged a look with Diana. We were both thinking that part of Adam's craziness might have had something to do with memories that he couldn't explain to himself but that had come up after he met me.

I dropped the subject of Adam and inquired about the woods altar. "It's a delightful place," Mattie said. "I'll have Rose take you there tomorrow, when the rain stops. They say it will be a clear day for our May Eve, with a full moon, too. The most exciting Beltane of my life! We'll be having our own private ceremony in the temple tomorrow, on the eve of the public dedication. That was when the pagans had it, you know. Christianized versions of the old festivals were displaced by twelve hours to the following day—a matter of different calendar systems: the older one lunar, the newer one solar. The pagans had reckoned their days from noon to noon; the Christians reckoned theirs from midnight to midnight."

Just after sunrise the next morning, Rose took me out to the woods altar. It lay in a small grove of pine trees not far from the house. As soon as I entered the grove, I felt the power of the place. In a circular space, outlined by tall trees, mist was rising from the damp earth in twisted veils, lanced by golden light. A shimmering beam haloed the small central altar built of old, mossy stones. Here and there around the circle stood effigies seven or eight feet high, roughly approximating human forms. One was a totem pole. One was a rough-hewn stone. One was a construction of driftwood, artfully entangled. One was a marble statue so eroded by time that few of its features were still discernible. One was a single tall column carved from black, glassy-looking rock. One was a massive log, five feet in diameter, set upright with a crude face, breasts, and yoni deeply cut into its side. Another upright log, almost as large, had the form and appearance of wood but had been transmuted into a solid mass of hard, agate-colored stone.

Rose blessed me with the pentacle and left me alone with these silent presences. I heard no sound except bird song. I approached the altar and laid my hands on it. (Diana had once told me that women were not allowed to do this in most of the man-made churches.) The old stones, warmed by the early sun, had a comforting feel.

I looked up, into the slanting path of light, and saw a single dark tree limned by silvery flashes. In the center of the tree, a face appeared. I gasped, because the face closely resembled the statue of the Black Goddess in the temple of Themiskyra.

The lips moved. I heard Her voice in my head. "Antiope, daughter, you have done well. Your mission is nearly finished. You have one more task to complete."

I fell to my knees, as much in surprise as in reverence. "Is it You, Mother?" I cried. I spoke in the mother tongue that I had not used for years. "Are You really here in this world, where I have been lost all this time?"

There was no reply, but the face seemed to incline toward me as a sudden breeze sprang up and stirred the tree. I was shaking with emotion. At last, a vision! After all the long months of struggling to learn while feeling abandoned and deprived of my own spiritual powers, I had found an image of the Goddess. It didn't matter whether it was within me or without. She was there. The woods altar seemed a holy place indeed.

I don't know how long I remained there, motionless, clutching the altar stones and breathing in the freshly rain-washed spring morning. When I looked up again, the sun was much higher. Its rays slanted much more steeply through the branches. I knew I should not stay too long away from the house. Mattie had arranged for a group of women to gather for an early lunch, followed by an afternoon tour of the new temple, and an evening ceremony "just for us," as she said.

Yet I was reluctant to leave the grove. I walked slowly around the circle and touched each one of the silent figures, holding my amulet bag in my other hand. Each figure provided a different, distinct inner sensation. Each seemed at home here, in a place created by the Mother Herself and not by human hands. Crude as they were, these icons of wood or stone seemed more meaningful than anything I had ever seen in those odd spiky structures that the people of this world called houses of God.

But I had not yet seen the fruition of Mattie's dream, the new house of the Goddess. This day, May Eve, which began with a vision, was to continue with revelation.

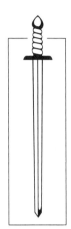

CHAPTER 13

THIRTY-NINE WOMEN MADE UP THE PARTY THAT VIS-
ited the temple that day. They were the same
women who had attended the Samhain ceremony
in Mattie's house, except for the elderly woman
with steel-rimmed glasses. We were told that she had died,
quietly and comfortably, of self-administered barbiturate poi-
soning, while some of the other women guarded her privacy.
Her place had been taken by the actress, Glinda Rivall. I recognized Glinda immediately; her face was often seen on television. Her eyes seemed pale and her skin blotchy, for today she
wore no makeup, but her well-known throaty voice was familiar
enough. Today her unpainted face claimed the same privilege
enjoyed by men in this world, to be accepted by all with whatever imperfections or blemishes might accompany their natural
appearance.

We traveled six miles to the temple site in three cars and
two vans, carrying robes and other paraphernalia. The temple
stood at one end of a wide street in the nearby town. As we
approached, we could see it soaring above the town's three- and
four-story buildings like a summer cloud soaring above the
horizon. It was a curve-sided pyramid of dazzling white stone.

Tall red entrance doors were deeply set in a pear-shaped yonic gateway.

Most of the other women had seen the place before, in various stages of completion, but all were impressed by its finished elegance. The vestibule was a large oval room whose curved walls converged upward to a water-green skylight, from which an aqueous glow bathed everything beneath. The underwater effect was further enhanced by darkly glittering, ripply silver patterns in the floor and wall tiles and by great branches of coral displayed along the walls. Double-tailed siren figures, carved of black onyx, stood in blue-lighted niches above the coral. Mattie had said that this entranceway represented the primal abyss, also called the Deep that existed before creation, a symbolic description of the Mother's womb.

We passed through a low, narrow, rounded doorway representing the gate of birth, through which we could fit only one at a time. This led to the main hall, an enormous round space with three upper galleries and a domed ceiling far above. On the ceiling was a stylized representation of the Goddess bending over, Her hands and feet carried all the way down to the floor through four heavy pillars set at the cardinal points. Her right and left hands marked the south and east, Her right and left feet the west and north. Her vast naked body was painted blue. From Her breasts flowed a Milky Way of stars, all picked out by small lamps. Various phases of the moon formed luminous decorations on Her belly. The sun, a large lighted globe, hung newborn between Her thighs. She was a modern version of the ancient Egyptian concept of the Sky Goddess, who touched the "ends of the earth" with Her fingers and toes. Here, the heavenly lights emanating from the Goddess's body were imitated by electricity.

This huge room was carpeted with thick cushions where people might sit or lie down to contemplate the immense figure overhead. Chairs were stacked around the walls, ready to be placed in any desired formation. In the middle of the hall was a small dais supported by caryatids carved from translucent red carnelian, like my Mother stone. Up along the galleries spotlights were hung that could illuminate any part of the room for rituals, lectures, or dramatic performances. Soft, meditative music from unseen speakers filled the space with pleasant sound. Mattie proudly pointed out the various features that made the great hall adaptable to many purposes.

Next she showed us through some of the temple's secular chambers. There was a fine library, with thousands of books, study tables, armchairs, and light streaming in through tall windows. There were classrooms, meeting rooms, consulting rooms, bathrooms, offices; a large banquet room with a fully equipped kitchen; a medical facility; a small theater; a nursery and children's playroom; an art gallery; a laboratory and a sauna. Mattie talked enthusiastically of the temple's readiness to serve many functions, like the Goddess temples of antiquity.

"The temple's most important function is, of course, spiritual," Mattie said, as we returned to the great hall. "I haven't yet showed you the primary symbols of spirituality here. I hope to present these symbols to you as the ancients did, in a deliberately created atmosphere of awe, as a personal experience aesthetically and sensually engendered for each of you. Some of you will become temple attendants and help others to receive such experiences. Today you will feel their power for yourselves, by entering what we call the labyrinth."

The entrance door of the labyrinth stood beside the right hand of the Sky Goddess, at the south pillar in the great hall. We were to enter this door singly, at two-minute intervals. Mattie said it was not a labyrinth to get lost in. Like the ancient ones, it had only one route, winding through the fabric of the building, up and down stairways and ramps, through tunnels and hidden chambers, emerging at last through a door at the left hand of the Goddess. Each visitor was to walk the labyrinth alone, so Mattie directed us to keep moving.

I was still waiting when the first woman emerged from the exit door and immediately sank to the floor. Some of us hurried over to her. She looked up, smiling, although her eyes glittered with tears. She was breathing hard, in the grip of strong emotion. She opened her mouth to speak, but Mattie put a finger on her lips and instructed, "Say nothing."

We watched as others came out the exit door. Each one seemed deeply moved. When my turn came, I touched my amulet bag, hitched my sword belt, and opened the door.

At first I was in a corridor of unrelieved darkness. Stretching out my hands to either side, I felt walls that seemed to be covered with velvet. I walked forward, turned several corners, and saw a dim light. Beyond an archway, a flight of stone steps led upward. The treads were worn down in the center, as if they had been constructed of very old stones.

I went up. On the first landing, in a pale blue light, a stone niche held the head and shoulders of a woman with snakes for hair. The figure startled me, it was so lifelike. The snakes moved and hissed quietly. The woman's eyelids suddenly opened wide, showing goatlike eyes with horizontal-slit pupils. Her lips opened. I heard a voice. It said, "You are approaching the first Mystery. Remember, you must kiss the stone."

I continued to climb. At the top of the stairs hung a filmy white veil, half concealing a diamond-shaped, closed door. I turned the knob and entered a small, dainty, pink and white bedroom, full of frills and ruffles. The bed was covered by a satin spread trimmed with lace, all white except for two things: a sprawled doll in a rose-colored gown and a long smear of blood. Real blood, with a real blood smell.

The bedroom had a window, but behind the pane there was nothing but a solid black wall. There was a door on the other side of the room: not diamond-shaped but oval, under a round arch. I crossed the room and opened this door. Now I found myself in a very low hallway, paneled in red brocade. Before me stood an elevator with open doors. I saw no other way out, so I stepped into the elevator. Its doors closed immediately, and it began to descend. There were no floor numbers inside it—in fact, no markings of any kind. Its walls were a flat, featureless gray.

When the elevator doors reopened, I stepped into a room that seemed to be padded with flesh-colored rubber. The floor and walls consisted of soft, springy hillocks. A long ramp led upward out of this room, to a very tight little corridor that twisted up and down, around and sideward, with slopes and steps, all in a dim rosy light. I could hear a soft music of harps and flutes.

Suddenly I turned a corner and entered what appeared to be the inside of a tower: a shaft of space reaching upward into darkness. In the center of this shaft stood a gigantic statue of a woman in a billowing blood-red robe, open over the bosom. Looking down, a knowing smile on her carved face, she cupped both hands under her breasts. Her eyes glittered like gems. Her realistic hair waved, along with the folds of her robe, in the warm air currents flowing upward from the floor. On top of her head, which towered at least twelve feet above the floor, sat a gleaming golden crown battlemented like the wall of an ancient city.

So sudden and so impressive was this apparition that I fell to my knees before her, for she closely resembled my concept of the Mother.

She opened her mouth, and a voice came: "Take the left-hand path."

I turned to my left and saw another small door, half hidden behind the statue. Set into the center of this door was a red stone the size and shape of a human heart. The door was closed and apparently locked. I twisted the doorknob in vain. Then I remembered the advice of the snake-haired effigy and put my lips to the stone. At once the door swung back. I faced a narrow ramp leading down into darkness. A musty odor came from this place. Below there were faint sounds, like sighing winds.

As I went down the ramp, I was nervous enough to keep my hand on the hilt of my sword. The door shut behind me with a bang, leaving me in darkness. The eerie sounds grew louder. The passage curled like a spiral around some unseen center, until its curve grew tighter and tighter and I saw light.

It was a flickering orange light, like fire. I passed around a final turn and came upon a cavern lit by dozens of candles in niches around the walls. The place seemed to be carved out of native rock deep in the earth—or if it was not, then it was an excellent imitation.

In the center of the cavern, on a dais of black onyx, stood a terrifying black Crone with four arms. She wore nothing but strings of pearls, gold beads, and a golden crown from which her long, uncombed gray hair flowed in stiff strings and ropes. Her eyes bulged like peeled grapes. Her lips grinned, showing pointed fangs. An impossibly long purple tongue hung out of her mouth, almost down to her breastbone. Her toenails and fingernails were curved talons, like a lion's claws. One of her hands bore a cup, one a wooden club, one a sword, and one a round disk inscribed with a pentacle. Under her feet lay a corpselike male homunculus.

All of this was so realistic that I suddenly remembered seeing a similar creature among pictures of museum artifacts. I almost, but not quite, could remember the name of the Crone Goddess who was so represented in a faraway country. I knew it contained the word Ma, which was a universally recognized sacred name among my people.

One of the gleaming black hands—the one holding the sword—slowly swung around to point toward an open stairwell on my right. A voice said, "If you climb beyond death, you will meet the essence of divinity. Do you dare remove the veil?"

I heard myself asking, in a whisper, "Are you Death?" There

was no reply. The sword pointed inexorably. I went cautiously around the wall of the chamber and began to climb the stairs.

As I went up, the darkness began to lift. I passed some small niches that shed a cool white light; each bore a symbolic object. One had a sprig of holly in a white vase. One held an ear of corn partly wrapped in a silk cloth. In another, there was a glass water jar containing a live fish. Another displayed a sphere of transparent polished quartz almost as big as my head. Another showed a large pentacle, more than a foot across, evidently cut from a thick plate of brightly polished copper.

The stairway was long, and the climb was tiring. The niches became larger, almost like windows through which came daylight, but they were covered by dead-white translucent panels that revealed nothing on the other side. The light was bright but unearthly, a white shadowless glow, like snowlight on a pale winter day.

The stairs ended at a hallway of strange perspectives. The floor was very wide at the beginning, but it rapidly narrowed. There was no ceiling. The side walls tilted inward and met overhead. At the narrow end of the hallway, there was a small door painted dead black, with another red heart stone set into its center. Silver letters circled around this stone. They said, "Beyond this door lies the veil of divinity. If you dare look behind the veil, you will see the Living Goddess."

This door also opened when I kissed the heart stone. I saw a short, straight corridor leading to another door marked "Exit." Hanging across the corner beside this door was the veil, of silvery spiderweb-gray silk, as big as a bedsheet, covering something. Apparently one could choose either to look behind the veil or to pass out of the exit without looking.

I paused only for a moment. Did I want to see the Living Goddess? Of course I did. I seized one edge of the veil and swept it aside.

There was nothing behind the veil but a full-length mirror.

Thoughtful and inexplicably moved, like the women who had preceded me, I came out of the exit door into the great hall, where the others were waiting. I felt that it would take me some time to sort out all the symbolism that I had seen in the labyrinth. I lay down on the cushions, stared up at the Sky Mother, and meditated on what I had seen and felt.

When each member of the group had taken the same journey and emerged from the same door, Mattie led us to another opening by the Goddess's left foot. "Now," she said, "we will enter the holy of holies. This place will be open only to those who have undergone a course of enlightenment, including the journey you have just taken."

Everyone kept silent as we walked through this final gate and down a broad corridor, lighted by lamps cleverly designed to resemble flaming torches in sconces along the walls. Mattie opened a set of double doors at the end and revealed a large chamber illuminated by a skylight high overhead. Here stood the colossal white marble statue of the naked Goddess, an extraordinary work of art, massive but graceful. It was not an idealized or stylized female form but one in which the ordinary dimensions of an average woman had been harmoniously blended into a beautiful composition. A shimmering length of emerald-green silk was draped over one of Her shoulders, falling to the floor at Her feet.

The Goddess stood at the northern side of a spacious round room, clearly designed for rituals to be performed by small groups. In the center of the room, a temporary wooden column had been set up, with long multicolored ribbons hanging from a flower-covered cone at its top. As Diana had described it to me, this was a traditional maypole, which long ago had represented the phallus of a god entering the body of the Goddess to fertilize Her afresh each springtime. My people had enacted the same annual Mystery but had not used a maypole.

The round chamber was lavishly decorated with flowers and potted plants, which put forth a sweet composite scent. Sprays of willow catkins stood in tall jade-green vases. At the Goddess's feet lay a number of brightly colored eggs, representing Her original Cosmic Egg from which universes were born and reborn.

Around the circumference of the sanctuary chamber there were seven doors, radiating off like spokes of a wheel. Mattie opened each door in turn to show us what lay beyond. The first was the door by which we had entered. The second led to a study and dressing room for the officiating priestess. The third opened into a music room, which could accommodate a small orchestra while its music was piped into both the sanctuary and the great hall. The fourth led to an extensive stockroom lined with shelves, which held such paraphernalia as robes, lights, candlesticks, seasonal decorations, spare furnishings, and so on.

The fifth door led to a remarkable meditation room, a hollow sphere designed to resemble the interior of a giant soap bubble, slightly flattened at the bottom. It was entirely lined with a soft translucent material, through which changing lights and rich rainbow colors constantly moved. I could imagine spending hours in that room, watching those beautiful shifting patterns until my consciousness drifted away into the dream world.

The sixth door led into the bottom of a round shaft, through which a spiral staircase rose up into darkness. Mattie said, "Those stairs go up through the temple's center to the tower room: a small, glass-enclosed chamber at the highest point of the building. The tower room is accessible only from here. From that room you have a broad view in every direction and also a clear view of the sky for night vigils and contemplations. The room is equipped with a telescope and star charts."

When she came to the seventh door, behind the statue of the Goddess, Mattie beckoned to me. She said, "For reasons that you'll soon understand, I want Ann to be the first to enter this door." She opened it, and I walked through. The door closed behind me.

I found myself in a short corridor resembling a cave. Before me there was a small yonic opening faced with red-dyed fleece, a large stone slab poised to cover it. Beyond the opening was a dark crawl passage, similarly lined with red fleece. I felt a sudden choking sensation. The hole so closely resembled the entrance to Themiskyra's womb chamber that for one desperate moment I thought I was home again.

Tears stung my eyes as I stooped into the tunnel and crawled down its length to the small space beyond. Sure enough, there was the softly lined chamber with its fresh-air vents, waste hole, and water source. It was all as I remembered it. I sat there weeping into my hands for several minutes before I regained sufficient control to crawl out again.

When I emerged from the passage into the sanctuary, I embraced Mattie, crying, "How did you know?"

She smiled. "Your description was very precise. Now please tell the rest of us what you saw."

I did so. Every woman nodded in recognition, for everyone had read Diana's book. While I sat down to center myself and restore my calm, the others went one at a time into the womb chamber to feel its atmosphere.

Mattie said, "We'll come back to the sanctuary this evening for our Beltane ritual. Now it's getting late, and a dinner is being prepared for us in the banquet room."

We were a rather sober group as we went in to that dinner. Each woman was mulling over her experience of the temple and sorting out her personal impression of the meanings of spirituality. I was frankly amazed by the job that Mattie's designers had done. This temple seemed as honest an expression of reverence for the Mother as any ever built by my own people, with this world's miracles of technology providing further enhancement.

It seemed truly a house of the Goddess. I remember hoping that it would indeed become a popular pilgrimage center for the spiritually deprived women of this world.

Nevertheless, my morning's vision at the woods altar stayed with me and nagged at the edges of my consciousness. What was my mission here? What could be meant by my final task? And if, as the temple mirror suggested, the sense of divinity was really myself speaking to myself, what did my inner being know that was still unrevealed to my ordinary perceptions?

I was to discover the truth of these matters all too soon.

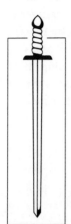

CHAPTER 14

AFTER A DELICIOUS MEAL AND A REST PERIOD, WE ALL returned to the sanctuary for the evening's ritual. We passed into the room one at a time, each making the sign of the pentacle as she entered. From the storeroom Mattie and Rose took green velvet cushions, flowing robes of green silk for us to wear, and thirteen green candles, which were lighted and placed around the foot of the maypole. Each woman laid her own talisman among these candles: doll, knife, cup, cards, photographs, various stones, jewelry, a book or two, some natural objects like sticks and shells, a stalactite from a cave, a wreath of dried grapevine, a handful of sheep's wool. I laid down an offering that was especially meaningful to me: an ornamental knot that I had made from black hairs combed out of Melanie's mane and tail.

For a while we sat together quietly, listening to soft music. Presently, four women arose and picked up the emblems of the cardinal points, calling upon the Goddess in the four directions, as was the custom of the group. When they resumed their seats, Mattie took a gorgeous silver chalice studded with colored gems, dipped her finger in it, and blessed the woman next to her, as was also the custom. When the cup came to me in its passage around the circle, I smelled a hint of woodruff in the liquid it contained and was able to identify it as May wine.

The article that next passed around the circle was a green willow wand, decorated with ribbons, for use as a talking stick. Mattie held it in hands that shook with emotion, as did her voice also. "I can hardly tell you what this night means to me," she said. "After all the years of dreaming and planning, now at last we are here in the first fully equipped Goddess temple to be erected in two thousand years of Western civilization. My personal vision quest ends here. This is what I was inspired to do.

"After tonight, the temple will be open to all, and strangers may freely enter. But tonight the doors are locked. We are alone in this place. It exists only for us. This will not happen again, ever, but I am most astoundingly happy that it is happening now. When the time comes for the Crone to take me away into Her darkness, I can say with honest pride that there was a reason for my having existed. This temple is the reason. May it outlive me, and all of us, by a thousand years at least."

Others murmured, "Hear, hear," and "Blessed be." Each woman, as the wand passed into her hands, blessed the temple and expressed a wish for its future. One woman said, "I want my grandchildren and their grandchildren to come here and learn." Another said, "From this center let a true sense of peace spread and spread, until all the world's aggressions and wars are swallowed up in the sisterhood of humanity."

Glinda, the actress, invoked the spirit of the old woman whose suicide had made a place for her in the circle. "She was a dear friend of mine," Glinda said, "and I know how happy she would have been if she could have lived to see this night. However, we would not have wanted her to live in pain, even to wait for this. I have put her picture on the altar, to give her a kind of attendance here in effigy. This whole day has been one of the most moving experiences of my life." Her voice choked with tears, and she hastily passed the wand on.

Diana said, "I too find this place and time filled with a promise that I would never have dreamed of, let alone hoped for, until I found Ann and began to write her story. How astonished I was to discover the hidden history of women in this civilization! What paths and byways of research I've traveled since! Now that those paths and byways have led me here, it feels like I've reached the end of a very long road that was neglected and overgrown but essential for me to find. I thank Mattie for bringing me here, and I thank Ann for showing me the way."

When her turn came, Rose opened a box and brought forth thirty-nine flower crowns that she had made for us to wear. She had worked on them for weeks, she said. They were gifts for each of us to keep and use in subsequent springtimes. These flowers would never fade. They were made of wire and silk, so artfully wrapped, stiffened, and colored that at a distance of a few feet one could hardly tell that they weren't real flowers. Rose said she had learned the art from her grandmother and wished to offer its products to the women's group as her own personal contribution. We all crowned ourselves with Rose's flowers.

Edith, who had been to Australia, also had gifts to distribute. From her trip she had brought back some small gemstones called opals, which showed remarkable flashes of different colors when they were turned different ways to the light. Mined from Australian rocks, they looked like what our priestesses called the Mother's "rainbow veils" of creation.

Edith gave one to each woman in the group and enjoined us all to keep them in sacred memory of this May Eve full-moon night, which would never occur again as we now experienced it. Some people in Australia, she said, maintained that a gift of a colorful opal occurred only once in a lifetime and represented a significant point in the lives of both giver and recipient.

I placed my opal in the bag with my amulet stones, vowing that I would never again be parted from it.

When the speaking was finished, Mattie withdrew to one side of the room and started a recording of music. She picked up a large drum to provide a percussive accompaniment. The rest of us pushed aside the cushions and took our places around the maypole, facing one another in couples, each holding an end of one of the thirty-eight ribbons.

"Now," Mattie directed, "if you do this tidily, the ribbons should end up nicely braided around the pole. The secret is to keep a uniform pace, and remember the over-and-under sequence. To start, each one walk forward and pass right shoulders with the person facing you, then left shoulders with the next, then right shoulders with the next, and so on around. Try to keep the ribbons fairly taut."

She began beating the drum in time with the music. The women began their maypole dance. I must say it was fun. The rhythm was infectious. I got into the spirit of the thing and began to leap and shout, as did others. By the time the maypole was braided (almost neatly) and all the ribbons had been used up, we were breathless with exertion, sweating, grinning, and thirsty.

Some of the women then produced cold bottles of wine and fruit juices with a stack of paper cups. Others brought out nuts, cheeses, and small wheat cakes. Sharing food with other women at the feet of a great white Goddess image felt wonderfully homelike and comforting to me. Already I was beginning to look upon this temple as a haven in this world where I was an eternally alien presence.

The others seemed to feel as good about it as I did. All were looking forward excitedly to the public dedication ceremonies on the morrow. A woman who lived nearby said that the town had been filling up with tourists, visitors, reporters, and television crews for the past three days. Many young people, both women and men, were camping out in vans, cars, tents, and sleeping bags around the local fields, waiting to enter the first

Goddess temple. Some of them had been calling themselves Goddess worshipers for years, even though there had never been any official recognition of their beliefs or any general acknowledgment of a movement embodying those beliefs.

We sat together until the candles burned low. Some of the women, who lived at greater distances, began to arise and bid the others good night. By ones and twos they drifted away, until the only ones left were those who had come in the van from Mattie's house. I spoke up then and asked if the others would wait long enough for me to visit the one spot in the temple that I had not yet seen: the tower room.

"Of course," Mattie said promptly. "Go along, Ann. Anybody else who feels like climbing those stairs is welcome to go, too. We'll wait for you. I don't want to tear myself away from the atmosphere of this place right away, anyhow. I can't seem to get enough of it."

No one else seemed sufficiently energetic to accompany me, so I went alone up the narrow spiral staircase to the tower room. Indeed, it was a very long staircase. Despite my strong legs and good wind, I was puffing when I arrived at the top.

The tower room was small and unlighted, but so bright was the full moon that I saw the tower's interior very well. The room was surrounded by glass on all sides, like the lantern of a lighthouse. In addition, a panel in the roof could be opened for the telescope, which was quite large. On a broad desk, flooded by moonlight, lay star charts, maps, and binoculars.

Standing nearly at the zenith, the moon poured down a light that was almost like daylight without colors. I picked up the binoculars and turned slowly around, looking at the town and the surrounding countryside in all directions. The headlights of an occasional car crawled across the scene. It was late. Only a few lights burned in the houses below. Sparse streetlights illuminated empty streets.

Suddenly my attention was caught by some movement in the street just in back of the temple. Three dark figures were stirring there, next to a parked delivery truck. They were doing something up close to the temple wall. One was bending over. Two others seemed to be carrying something. They came together and conferred; then one got into the cab of the delivery truck. The other two disappeared from my sight beneath the curve of the building. After a few minutes they reappeared and got into the truck. Headlights flashed on, and the truck drove away.

This was puzzling. Who could those people have been, and what were they doing? If they were technicians setting up speakers or cameras for tomorrow's ceremony, they were in the wrong place. If they were removing trash or delivering supplies, they were doing it at a peculiar time. I wondered about it as I left the tower room and descended the long stair. I thought I might ask Mattie if any night deliveries were expected, but when I rejoined the others, the conversation had turned to other things, and I forgot.

Just before we left the now-darkened great hall, my eye caught one other peculiar thing. On the floor near the doorway, half hidden under a stack of chairs, lay a small bundle of rods that I thought I had seen somewhere before but that I could not identify. I was lagging behind. Mattie was calling to me to hurry so she could lock the door. I spent only a moment or two on the effort to place that odd-looking little bundle. What was it? Where had I seen something like it before?

Oh, yes, I should have remembered: after all, I had gained a large percentage of my information about this culture from watching television. I knew what those things looked like; they were just not familiar enough to me to identify them easily. By the time it dawned on me, it was almost too late.

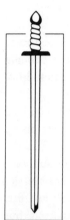

CHAPTER 15

DEDICATION DAY DAWNED FAIR AND BRIGHT. ALL THE members of Mattie's household planned to attend the ceremony and seemed excited about it, though not all of them held personal convictions in favor of the Goddess. Even the unconvinced, however, seemed to be motivated by genuine liking and respect for their employer.

A caravan of vehicles set off for the temple site shortly after sunrise. A crowd was already gathering in the street before the temple, which shone like a pearl in the sunlight. Television trucks were parked along the curb. A bank of microphones had been set up before the entrance, where speakers and singers would appear.

When the ceremony began, the crowd grew quiet. A chorus of women sang one of the Goddess chants, and some of the audience joined in. The mayor of the town introduced Mattie, who spoke about the realization of her dream in the unique design of this building. "We didn't want to copy the style of traditional churches," she said, "but rather to express a feminine image with curved lines and rounded spaces. There were many technical difficulties involved in this kind of construction. The architects and builders came up with ingenious solutions to the problems and helped to create a true aesthetic enhancement of the area. I hope this temple will serve the town well and bring it honor for many years to come."

This was greeted with a patter of applause and some cheering. I caught a few other voices—harsh, heckling ones—in the back of the crowd, but their words were indistinct.

Three ministers of local churches spoke, having been invited especially to forestall reactionary criticism. Although they showed a tendency to damn with faint praise, they were obviously trying to sound fashionably ecumenical and tolerant. One said, "It is to be hoped that this new sect will lead the women of our community to a deeper understanding of spiritual life, that they may be led toward the universal Deity we all revere." The second one also described the Goddess religion as a "sect" and proposed that a union of the theological concepts of God and Goddess might support a more egalitarian society. The third one talked about a Mother God. Not one even mentioned the possibility of altogether replacing the God concept with the Goddess concept nor was anything said about men attending the temple.

Glinda Rivall gave some selected readings from Diana's book and other sources, speaking of the antiquity and vitality of the Goddess in the original development of ethical systems and human values. Her rich, dramatic voice rolled mellifluously over the crowd, carrying conviction.

Looking out over the sea of faces, I saw many receptive smiles. I also saw something else that gave me a jolt in the belly, as keenly physical as if I had been suddenly punched: I saw Adam.

I saw him because he was in motion, threading his way deliberately through the crowd, heading for the side street. Something about his motion looked furtive. He was trying hard to be inconspicuous. This made me feel uneasy. Something was wrong. I felt compelled to follow him.

Hiding behind the shoulders of onlookers so the cameras wouldn't find me, I slid carefully down from my perch on one of the temple's front steps. I waited in the shadow of the balustrade, my face turned to the wall. When Adam emerged from the crowd and turned the corner into the side street, I cautiously followed.

He was moving faster now, like one with a definite destination. Without looking back, he turned another corner, making for the alley at the rear of the temple. With a sudden pang of apprehension, I realized that this was the place where I had seen dark figures doing something the night before.

I stopped at the corner and slowly peered around the curve of the building. I saw Adam's back. He was bending over one of the large trash cans at the curb, lifting something out of it. From his posture, I judged that it was something heavy. He set it down on the sidewalk and squatted in front of it. After a few minutes he stood up and reached toward one of the temple windows, which was slightly open. He was handling a long wire.

All at once I understood the meaning of the bundle of rods I had glimpsed, the reason for Adam's furtive behavior, the dire and dangerous craziness of what he was doing at this moment. Fanatic that he was, he intended to destroy the temple in the very sight of all the world that cared to watch—and perhaps to destroy many lives along with it.

I felt that there was not a moment to lose. Snatching my sword out of its sheath, I ran down the alley toward him, crying, "Stop!"

He half turned toward me, a startled expression on his face. Then he quickly turned back to his task, trying to connect or fix something before I could reach him.

When I did reach him, I seized his shoulder with all my strength and flung him back against the wall of the temple. Having been off balance, squatting on his heels, he sprawled and hit the concrete hard. I saw what he had been working on:

a black box from which several twisted wires led through the open window into the temple.

I stood over Adam with my sword in hand while he shook his head and glared up at me. "What do you think you're doing?" he snapped.

"What do you think *you're* doing?" I cried. "You're committing a crime!"

"This is God's work," he said grimly. "You'll have to kill me to stop me. Will you do that? Will you run me through with your witch's sword?"

He was calmly defiant, sure of himself, fearless. In his face, I saw again those golden eyes of the dying man before whom I had stood, long ago, with my sword in hand.

For a moment the temple, the sidewalk, all my surroundings seemed to waver and fade, to be replaced by the shadows of a battlefield where swords rang and clashed. Adam lay before me in the uniform of a Greek soldier. I didn't want to kill him.

The half-formed vision distracted me. I couldn't see what he was doing. Suddenly he sprang up at me. There was a knife in his hand. He slashed my sword arm and shoved me down into the gutter. My sword went tumbling and clanging along the pavement.

Adam turned quickly and leapt up to seize the open window and pull himself through. While I lay staring at my bleeding arm, he disappeared into the temple.

I knew I must follow him at any cost. My sense of his mind told me that he would willingly kill himself if the temple could be destroyed at the same time. I realized that there could be a way for him to set off the charges from inside the building. I thought of running back to my friends for help, but it seemed a waste of precious—and perhaps crucial—time. Seizing my sword with my left hand, I climbed through the window.

I could hear him going through passages and storerooms, following the wires. He wasn't bothering to keep quiet. He didn't know I was behind him. I kicked off my shoes and went after him silently. I caught up with him just as he reached the great hall.

I slipped around the doorpost and took aim at his back. At the last instant, he heard me and tried to twist aside. Because I was using my weaker hand and perhaps also because I really didn't want to harm him, my blade struck no vital spot but only sliced the muscle at his side. Blood stained his shirt and he staggered, but he didn't fall. He turned quickly to face me, knife in hand.

"All right, come on, Amazon," he said through clenched teeth. "Let's see how good you are. You've got the advantage of a longer blade."

"Please, don't fight," I begged him. "Why should we hurt one another? I mean you no harm, and neither does this temple. Why do you want to destroy something beautiful and your own life with it?"

"Beautiful isn't always good," he said. "This place is evil. I'm the one chosen to destroy the evil." As he said this, I realized that he was quite mad. His eyes had a fixed, glassy look. His fingers were twitching. He seemed to be speaking to himself, no longer aware of me; but then he jumped at me, nearly catching me off guard. He was quick. He slashed at me again with his knife. I saw that at some time in his life he had learned a rough and relentless fighting style. I parried his blow and jabbed him again. We circled each other warily.

He was right; I did have the advantage of a longer blade. I was able to thrust inside his defense. I cut the pectoral muscle and then the deltoid muscle of the arm that held his knife. As that arm fell useless to his side, he swiftly transferred the knife to his other hand. Then he turned and ran from me, leaving a trail of blood. He blundered into the door of the labyrinth, clawed it open, and disappeared within.

Now, I thought, I had him. He couldn't get at the explosives in the great hall. But could there be more of them, inside the labyrinth? That was an anxious thought.

From the slather of blood that he left in his wake, I judged that he might be bleeding to death, but it might be a long while before he was seriously weakened. What damage might he do? In a fever of distress, I paused long enough to slice a strip of fabric from one of the cushions and knot it around my injured arm. Then I followed him into the labyrinth.

To walk into the pitch-dark corridor knowing that a wounded, homicidal enemy lurked somewhere ahead was intensely frightening. I rolled my feet down slowly and tried to quiet my breathing, to be as silent as if I were not there at all. Still, I had to keep an elbow against one wall in order to feel my way, and that made a faint sound. I expected at any moment to feel a body launched against me and a blade in my heart. My ears felt literally strained with the effort of listening for nearly inaudible stirrings in the darkness.

After turning some corners, I saw light gradually brightening ahead and perceived that the corridor was empty except for a ragged line of blood splotches on the floor. Nevertheless, I slid slowly around each corner with painful caution.

The blood spoor showed me that he was beginning to stagger. Here and there the walls were smeared where he had lurched into them. At one point a handprint on the wall was dragged down to a fair-sized puddle on the floor, showing that he had fallen. The trail led up the stone stairway, past the snake-haired gorgon, and through the diamond-shaped door, which stood open.

The white veil had been ripped down from the doorway and torn apart. A blood-spotted remnant lay bundled in a corner. I entered the pink and white bedroom and found it a shambles. The bedclothes had been pulled from the bed. Delicate glass bottles and jars on the dressing table were broken. The mirror was cracked. Instead of one startling smear of blood on the virginally white bed, there were streaks of blood everywhere.

Very carefully, I bent and looked under the bed. He was not there, and there was no other place of concealment. I went on through the other door and picked up the blood trail, leading down the red brocade corridor and into the elevator, where there was a large red pool. Clearly, the elevator had carried him down to the lower level.

I went down and continued to follow his trail through the padded room and the twisted tunnel into the shaft where the huge red-clothed Goddess stood. Here the trail ended. I saw him lying in a heap against the other door, one hand reaching up toward the doorknob, apparently too weak to rise. He had not heard the gorgon's voice; he didn't know how to open the door. He was trapped.

He heard me coming. His eyes slanted toward me, showing a gleam of madness. He raised his head feebly and spoke in a husky whisper. "OK, you win. You've got me now. Are you going to kill me?"

"Not if I don't have to," I said. "I want you to live. I want you to be well. Will you let me help you?"

He grinned without humor. "Sure you can help me. Do you know the way out of here?"

"Yes."

"I can't walk anymore," he said. "I'll have to lean on you."

"First throw your knife over here."

He did so. The knife clattered across the stone floor and fetched up at the feet of the Goddess. I approached him, sheathed my sword, and pulled him up by his good arm. His knees were buckling. I put my arm around his back and propped him on my shoulder. I opened the door and dragged him down the dark spiral ramp, my legs shaking with the effort to support his weight.

His head lolled against mine. Somewhere in the darkness he turned his face toward me and kissed my cheek, whispering into my ear, "I love you." Those were his last words.

In the candlelit cavern of the Crone I felt his good hand fumbling at my sword hilt. Burdened as I was, I couldn't react fast enough to prevent him from pulling the sword out of its sheath and jabbing me in the side. Galvanized with sudden pain, I shoved him away. He fell like a sackful of rocks. His head banged against the corner of the black onyx dais. The sword fell to the floor.

Perhaps it was because of the years when I had no longer functioned as a true warrior, or perhaps it was because of my powerful attraction to him, but in truth I thought of his injury before my own. I fell to my knees beside him and raised his head. His eyes were open and motionless. His neck flopped limply. I felt at his throat for a pulse and found none.

He was dead.

All at once my heart was hurting almost as much as the wound in my side. I rocked back and forth in pain. I looked up at the threatening face of the four-armed black Crone and knew that She was Death indeed. I said, "Mother, look on Your spring-time sacrifice. Your temple has been anointed with blood. Is that what You wanted?"

Tears were rolling down my cheeks.

That I should have twice slain this man, whose fate seemed tragically linked with mine, was an irony that I could hardly bear. I went on speaking to the statue, just as if She could really hear me.

"Perhaps he was mad, but it may have been the fault of this bitter and hostile world. At heart, I think, he was kind. The animals knew that of him. So did I. If anything here is evil, it's the endless artificial rivalry that makes cruel lunatics of men who should be kind. Mother, why should I be the agent of his death? I didn't want this."

Hardly in control of myself, I straightened out Adam's body on the black dais, folded his arms, and closed his eyes. I leaned over the dead face and smoothed back the hair. I began to wail, echoing my foremothers' ancient, traditional ululation for the dead.

After a long while, I groped for my sword and staggered to my feet. I felt very weak. There was only one place where I wanted to be now: the womb chamber, so like Themiskyra's cave. As a wounded animal wants to go straight to its den, I wanted to go straight to that darkness and silence.

Before I left the cavern, I looked back: Adam lay in front of the homunculus at the Goddess's feet. She stood above him, poised in Her arrested dance of death, indifferent as the earth that casually soaks up blood, cold as the stone to which ten thousand years of life's agony is the same as no time at all. The ineffable sadness of the scene struck me as a final truth — perhaps the only final truth. Fighting and striving and hating — yes, and loving too — all came to nothing in the end but an eternal stillness at the feet of the Black Goddess.

Slowly I climbed the long stairway, leaving now my own trail of blood. My legs were becoming so weak that I feared I would collapse before reaching the womb chamber. I didn't look again into the mirror of the Living Goddess, culmination of the teaching of the labyrinth. I knew what I would see in that mirror: a weary woman in bloodstained clothing with a lost look in her eyes.

I fell once at the exit door and found it hard to get up again. I crossed the great hall, entered the sanctuary, and fell again before I reached the seventh door behind the statue. I was crawling by the time I arrived at the yoni entrance to the fleece-lined tunnel. I pulled myself through it and into the farthest corner of the womb chamber, and there I huddled in the dark, curled up as tightly as possible, with my arms around my knees.

My last conscious thoughts were of my women friends and how they managed to live in this world, and cope with it, and sometimes even flourish in it. For myself, I felt a bleak defeat and a draining away of my former warrior pride. What had that pride brought me except bloodstained hands and a disappointed heart? Was it really possible to win peace by violence? I had never questioned this premise before, but now my faith in the warrior's code was shaken.

With a wounded mind as well as a wounded body, I withdrew into immobility and silence and thus passed into unconsciousness.

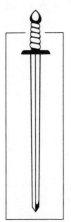

CHAPTER 16

WHEN I RECOVERED CONSCIOUSNESS, IT WAS TO FIND that someone was with me, drawing me with firm but gentle hands toward the gateway of the womb chamber. Behind this person's dark shape there were gleams of light at the other end of the passage and the sound of voices. Female voices.

Partly urging and partly pulling, my companion induced me to crawl sluggishly through the passage toward the light. At the entrance, women's hands took hold of me and drew me forth, as the hands of a midwife priestess draw forth an infant from its mother's body. I was helped to my feet and supported, while my eyes tried to focus on the face that swam in a haze before me.

A voice said, "Antiope, be at peace. You are safe." It was my mother tongue.

My eyes cleared, and I gazed with astonishment on a face that I had seen years ago, in what I had begun to think of as a dream: the face of the priestess at Themiskyra, the last face I had looked upon in my old home.

Now I looked about wildly. Other priestesses were there, holding torches. I was not in the sanctuary of Mattie's Goddess temple but in the ancient cave hollowed out of Mother Earth

Herself. Holy women surrounded me. I looked down at my body. My clothes had vanished. I wore only my amulet bag and my sword belt. There was no wound in my side. There was no bandage on my arm.

And the air smelled different. Even in the depths of this cave, it was a sweeter air than I had breathed for several years.

Overcome by a combination of physical weakness and emotional shock, I burst into tears and wept aloud, leaning on the shoulder of the priestess. When I grew quieter, I was led by slow steps to another chamber of the temple, where the women bathed me, massaged me, and fed me warm milk in token of my new birth.

Gradually, I began to recover my strength.

When I felt well enough to speak of my vision, priestesses and clansisters gathered to hear my tale and to record it. I talked for many days, hours each day. On the fourth day my mother arrived, accompanied by my sisters and my Aunt Leukippe. I fell into their arms. With their dear faces before my eyes at last, I was so deeply moved that I was unable to proceed with my story that day.

To my surprise, I found myself a great celebrity in the clan. The high priestess consulted with her spirit and came to the conclusion that the Mother had vouchsafed me a vision of genuine prophecy, despite its unbelievable features. The very grotesqueness of that world, she said, proved that it could be no human invention. Not even the most eccentric dream could create such unnatural details. It followed, then, that the Goddess had given me a picture of a real future — an idea that I found terrifying.

Would such a society actually exist someday, to despoil and poison our blessed earth and to torment its inhabitants both animal and human?

Sometimes in the middle of the night I awoke and wept, having seen again the shades of my brave friends from that world, missing my adopted mother Diana, wondering if she would actually live a life from which I would suddenly vanish as abruptly as I had arrived. We had grown close, Diana and I. It would be sad for her to find me and then to lose me.

Sometimes I fancied that I could hear again some of the unnatural sounds that I had become used to in that world: highway traffic, jet engines, strange music, or the more intimate purring of a refrigerator or the ticking of a clock. Sometimes I awoke, thinking I heard a telephone ring. I missed the convenience of instant hot water, electric light, prepackaged food, washing machines, and indoor plumbing. I even missed television, though not for long.

The joy of being restored to my motherclan gradually overcame my nostalgia for those indulgences and luxuries. I re-adapted myself to the harder but warmer life of my own people. I even forgot most of the language that I had learned in that other world. The words faded from my memory with astonishing rapidity. One day I suddenly said to myself the word *airplane* and couldn't remember what it meant.

One thing I never forgot, though: the haunting thought that the broken, corroded sword in Mattie's museum collection was no mere twin of my sword but the very same one.

Eventually I decided that even if my vision had shown a real future, or one possibility of a real future, still it was but a dream encountered in trance; it was not real now and perhaps would not be real ever.

My life settled down. I took a new lover, a smith by trade, and considered making him the father of my daughters in the near future. He was intelligent, kind, and a very competent craftsman.

I began raising a new filly to replace my lost Windeater. She was a pretty little chestnut with very long legs. I named her Sunrunner. Because Sunrunner was not yet old enough to be ridden, my sister Niobe sometimes loaned me her yellow stallion when I wanted a mount. Early one morning, I took him and rode out to the high meadow where our warriors had fought the last battle against the Greeks.

There I found the funerary mound that had been raised over our honored dead, and the other mound—shunned, overgrown, and neglected—under which the Greek dead had been piled together. I made a brief obeisance to the former and proceeded toward the latter. My purpose was to leave a courtesy offering there for the spirit of the man I had killed—twice. The atonement I had made in the womb chamber (or both womb chambers) seemed adequate to appease his spirit and render it approachable.

I dismounted from the horse and left him quietly cropping the grass on the former battlefield, now peacefully green as if no battles had ever been fought.

I approached the rough mound under which Greek bodies lay rotting. I pictured the golden-eyed soldier in my mind's eye and saw even more vividly his otherworld twin, Adam. What had the Goddess meant by throwing these two incarnations of one man into my experience? In that later time, we had almost loved one another. Would there be another time and place beyond that, where we might meet in peace and find real love?

I meant to give up to the earth that enclosed him one of my precious amulets, the golden eye stone, to represent my hope that clear sight would come to us both, dispelling the darkness that had shadowed our meetings. I was thinking of Adam as I opened the pouch and poured out my sacred stones into the palm of my hand.

I stared down at them in astonishment. There were not four stones anymore. There were five.

The fifth one was a small multicolored opal from a faraway place that would someday be named Australia. It was the stone that resembled the rainbow veils of the Goddess, concealing ultimate reality. As I held it in my hand, the scene flashed vividly into my mind: a group of women not yet born, sitting in a circle within the sanctuary of a temple not yet built, at the feet of a Goddess image not yet imagined. I saw Edith distributing her gifts, telling of the sacred red mountain and the strange animals that carried their young in body pockets. I heard her saying that the gift of an opal is given only once in a lifetime, and I heard myself vowing that I would never be parted from this stone but would keep it in memory of a May Eve night of the full moon, a night that would never occur again.

Or would it?

The scene lay in my past, but was it in the world's future?

The reality of this stone in my hand shook my faith in everything.

Perhaps my experience had only been a warning from the Goddess, to show that we must not allow our world to take those directions. Perhaps She meant me to record my experience so that our descendants might prevent the development of such a world. But could it be prevented by killing Adam?

I buried my golden eye stone in the earth, over the bones of a golden-eyed warrior. Then I mounted the horse and rode back home.

▼   ▼   ▼